David Taylor

111 Places
in Northumberland
That You
Shouldn't Miss

T0243827

emons:

Guidebooks for Locals & Experienced Travellers
Join us in uncovering new places around the world at
www.111places.com

Foreword

The ancient Kingdom of Northumbria was *huge*. At its greatest extent it included what is now Northumberland, Cumbria, County Durham and Yorkshire, as well as a good chunk of the Scottish Borders. The modern county of Northumberland isn't *quite* so big – it no longer stretches to the Humber for one thing; the River Tyne now defines the county's southern boundary (with the Tweed performing a similar service in the north). Northumberland hasn't included Newcastle since 1400 either (though, for the purposes of this book, I've cheekily inserted the city back into the county). Northumberland is still a big place though, stretching roughly 70 miles from top to bottom and 45 miles at its widest.

Within Northumberland's borders you'll find rugged and wild rolling hills, arable farmland, friendly market towns and characterful villages. The county is stuffed to the brim with history too. There are Iron Age hillforts, numerous Roman remains, including a long stretch of Hadrian's Wall, medieval castles and bastles, as well as sites associated with the Industrial Revolution. And the county has a beautiful and varied coastline, one that is largely unspoiled and a haven for both holiday makers and wildlife.

The 111 places in this book isn't – could never be – a definitive list. It could quite easily have been 222 or even 333 (there really is a *lot* to see in Northumberland). Some of the places featured in the following pages had to go in (Bamburgh Castle is as a tourist destination unmissable, but also – thanks to its lofty eminence on the Northumberland coast – unmissable). However, some places were chosen simply because I liked them, and I wanted other people to discover and like them too (the Cheviot Hills are wonderfully atmospheric, yet strangely overlooked). Hopefully this book is all the encouragement you need to go out and experience the delights of Northumberland for yourself.

111 Places

1 Lead Mining
Pencil a visit in

Allenheads doesn't look like an industrial powerhouse, but looks can be deceiving. For nearly 300 years the village's lead mine was a profitable and busy enterprise, one of the most important in the area. The mine closed in 1896, but traces of it can still be seen simply by walking around the village and knowing where to look.

Lead was extracted from seams of granite, which formed some 290 million years ago. Mineral-rich fluids seeped along cracks in the rock, eventually solidifying to leave veins of lead ore and fluorite. The first mines were probably dug in the 16th century, but it wasn't until the 18th and 19th centuries that lead mining in and around Allenheads reached its peak.

Like all mining work, extracting lead ore was a physically demanding occupation. Next to a road junction is the Gin Hill Mine Shaft, a 240-foot vertical drop deep underground. Miners made their way to the pit workings by climbing down a series of ladders (and then back up them at the end of their shift…). Across the road is another mine entrance, but one designed for ponies. Instead of ladders, the ponies followed a winding spiral incline downwards. The ponies were used to haul tubs of lead ore to the mine shaft, where it would be winched to the surface.

Not everything in Allenheads involved manual labour, however. Inside its own display building is a twin cylinder double-acting hydraulic engine, designed by Lord Armstrong and built in 1846. It was powered by water from two reservoirs above Allenheads, and was used to power machinery in the mine's workshops, including a lead ore crusher, as well as the saw mill.

Next to a car park are a series of now-abandoned stone buildings. The freshly extracted lead ore was brought to a washing floor there, so that the ore could be sorted and impurities washed out. From there the ore would be taken away for smelting.

Address Northumberland, NE47 9HD | Getting there Bus 688 Tynedale Links to War Memorial or Inn; small free car park near The Allenheads Inn | Tip Thorngreen Lime Kilns are further evidence of Allendale's industrial past. The twin kiln structure is thought to be one of the largest in the region.

2 — Ferryman's Hut
Small, but perfectly formed

Directly across the River Aln from the village of Alnmouth is Church Hill. To go from one to the other requires a *very* long detour, both when driving or walking. The Ferryman's Hut in Alnmouth is evidence that there was once another option: a ferry. For more than 60 years, a succession of ferrymen rowed passengers back and forth across the Aln. The last of these was a retired fisherman called John Brown. The hut was used by ferrymen as an equipment store, one vital part of which was a fish box, onto which passengers could step as they climbed into the ferry (the only rule stipulated by the Duke of Northumberland – who granted permission for the ferry service – was that passengers should never need to take their shoes off or get their feet wet). The ferry was mainly used by tourists, and largely during the summer months. Demand for the service ceased when beach huts on the Church Hill side were pulled down at the end of the 1960s.

The Ferryman's Hut is now a museum showing local memorabilia, as well as archive photos of the ferrymen. Perhaps the most heart-warming photo in the collection is that of a smiling Brown in his boat, with a happy passenger sitting next to him and obviously enjoying the experience. Wonderfully, the Ferryman's Hut qualifies as the smallest museum in Northumberland, and possibly even in the UK. (Effectively just a modified garden shed, the hut only has room inside for a handful of people at a time.)

That a ferry was needed to reach Church Hill was due to a violent storm that rolled in on Christmas Day, 1806. The storm caused the Aln to change course, cutting Church Hill off from the village. This led to the rapid decline of Alnmouth as a commercial harbour. Alnmouth was saved financially by the building of a railway line, which brought in holidaymakers. They, ironically, then needed a ferry to reach their beach huts on the quieter side of the river.

Address The Ferry Hut Museum, Riverside Road, Alnmouth, Northumberland, NE66 2RY | Getting there Bus 418 to Schooner Hotel and then a short walk; train to Alnmouth and then a 26-minute walk (or take the 418 bus from the nearby Curly Lane stop); limited free parking on Riverside Road or paid parking at Alnmouth Car Park and then a 10-minute walk | Hours Opened every day by a villager | Tip The Schooner is a 17th-century coaching inn serving food and drink, as well as providing accommodation. There are said to be some 60 ghosts haunting The Schooner, leading to its naming as the 'Most Haunted Hotel in Britain' (www.theschoonerhotel.co.uk).

3 Guano Shed

Where there's muck, there's brass

The word guano has a wonderfully round sound that really rolls off the tongue. Spanish in origin, it *should* be the sort of word that helps to reveal a profound and universal truth about human existence. Something like 'Guano is certainly the finest balm for the pangs of disappointed love', for instance. What holds the word back from popular usage is the fact that guano is an accumulated mass of seabird (or bat) excrement. (This helps to explain the otherwise puzzling omission of the term in the works of Jane Austen.)

Guano was once a very valuable commodity indeed. It's particularly rich in elements such as potassium, phosphate and nitrogen. These useful chemicals help to replenish soils that have been overworked and are lacking in nutrients. Huge deposits of guano were discovered on islands off the coast of Peru in the early 19th century. This sparked an acquisitive scramble by Western powers once it was realised how useful guano could be. In 1858, Great Britain imported over 300,000 tons of the stuff, for instance.

Some way south of Alnmouth and the River Aln are the remains of a Victorian guano shed, where guano would have been stored. The shed is some distance from the village for a *very* good reason: the smell of decaying bird poop must have been horrendous. (Take a moment to sympathise with the poor sailors who transported the guano to Alnmouth in the first place. Spending time at sea with such a pungent cargo can't have been fun…). The shed was probably in use for a very short period, however: the 'Guano Era' largely came to an end during the War of the Pacific, which kicked off in 1879. By this point, Peruvian deposits of guano were much depleted thanks to overexploitation. And artificial fertilisers had been developed that were cheaper too, making guano less economically viable. The Alnmouth shed is a ruin now, and was last used as a command post and pill-box during World War II.

Address Riverside Road, Alnmouth, Northumberland, NE66 2RY | Getting there Bus 418, X18 Max or X20 Max to Curly Lane and then a 40-minute walk; train to Alnmouth and then a 40-minute walk; limited parking in a lay-by near Waterside Cottages and then a 30-minute walk | Hours On private land but viewable from the Northumberland Coast Path / St Oswald's Way | Tip Just a few minutes' walk north of the guano shed is the triangular mound of Church Hill, from which there is a splendid view of Alnmouth across the River Aln. A ruined 19th-century mortuary chapel can be found to the west of the hill.

4 Alnwick Castle
Star of the silver screen

Alnwick Castle is the ancestral home of the Dukes of Northumberland and is widely known as the 'Windsor of the North'. (Or should Windsor be dubbed the 'Alnwick Castle of the South'? Discuss.) The castle was founded in the 11th century as a stronghold and power base for Norman nobleman Ivo de Vesci. The border with Scotland is a mere 19 miles away, so building a castle was an eminently sensible idea.

Unfortunately, Alnwick Castle was captured by the Scots under King David I in 1136, and besieged by King William IV in 1173 and again in 1174. In 1212, Eustace de Vesci, Ivo's great grandson, was accused of plotting against the English King John and, ironically, fled to Scotland. Eustace was a leader in the Barons' War, which eventually led to the signing of the Magna Carta, the foundation of England's common law.

In 1253, presumably to the dismay of the de Vescis, King Henry III passed ownership of Alnwick Castle to Antony Bek, who later became Bishop of Durham. Bek sold the castle on to the Percy family, in whose hands it has remained. The impressive stone castle that stands today is largely the work of the Percys, starting with Henry Percy and continuing with his son, also Henry.

The grandeur of Alnwick Castle has not been lost on film and TV producers. It has been used as the location for an impressive number of productions over the years. The most high-profile were the first two *Harry Potter* movies, with the castle standing in for Hogwarts School of Witchcraft and Wizardry, attended by Harry. Alnwick Castle is also the fictional Brancaster Castle, home of Lord Hexham, in the popular TV series *Downton Abbey*. And Edmund Blackadder, played by Rowan Atkinson, failed to stay on a horse in front of the castle in the closing titles of *The Black Adder*, broadcast in 1983. Funny? Even a stone-faced Norman earl would laugh.

Address Alnwick, Northumberland, NE66 1NQ, +44 (0)1665 511100,
www.alnwickcastle.com | Getting there Bus 473, X15 Max, X18 Max, 418 and various
others to Alnwick Bus Station and then a short walk; paid parking at Alnwick Castle
and Gardens Car Park | Hours Mar–Oct daily 10am–5.30pm | Tip Edlingham
Castle has been voted one of the top three castles in Northumberland, and was once
a Percy home. A ruin now, it's notable for its apparently gravity-defying leaning tower
(www.english-heritage.org.uk).

5 Bondgate Tower
Breathe in

Bondgate Tower is the last original remnant of a 15th-century town wall built to protect Alnwick from attacks by Scottish raiders. Of the other three towers, only the Pottergate Tower still stands, though that was extensively rebuilt in a gothic style in the 18th century. The Clayport and Narrowgate Towers – as well as the wall itself – are long gone.

The tower is the eastern gateway into the centre of town, with the main road passing through a stone archway. Handsome as the Bondgate Tower is, it was clearly never designed for modern traffic. There's a height restriction on vehicles for one thing, so tall vans are a squeeze, and lorries are a definite no. The road narrows to one lane too. During the tourist season this leads to long queues, so canny drivers park outside and walk into town.

Remarkably, people were complaining about this situation in the 19th century. According to *The History of the Borough, Castle, and Barony of Alnwick*, written by George Tate and published in 1866, 'Utilitarians would complain that this ancient gateway is a nuisance and would have it taken down, because it is not large enough to allow a free passage to large vehicles, such as caravans'. Bondgate Tower did have a supporter in Tate, though, as he also wrote 'Earnestly, do we hope that this brave old tower may be carefully preserved' and that 'although grim and weatherworn…' is a '…picturesque object, stirring up ancient memories of brave men and heroic deeds, which throw a glory around the town…'.

Despite the clear and prominent modern warning signs, some drivers still attempt to take oversized vehicles through. This has caused damage to the stonework in the recent past, requiring the road to be closed to traffic so that repairs could be carried out. But, for all the inconvenience, what finer way to enter a town is there than through the gateway of a medieval tower?

Address Bondgate Within, Alnwick, Northumberland, NE66 1SX | Getting there Bus 473, X15 Max, X18 Max, 418 and various others to Alnwick Bus Station and then a short walk; parking at Greenwell Road (Part A) Car Park (requires parking disc available from Alnwick's Tourist Information Centre and some local shops) | Tip The renovated Alnwick Playhouse is arguably the cultural centre of the town, and has a wonderfully varied programme of film shows, theatre productions and concerts (www.alnwickplayhouse.co.uk).

6 — Dirty Bottles
Leave well alone

Cleaning can be hazardous to your health. Muscle strain, cuts and bruises are common, as are sprains, infections, and – if you're particularly keen on keeping dirt under control – repetitive strain injury. Cleaning can result in conditions such as tendonitis, lateral epicondylitis and torn ligaments. That's not all: the chemicals found in some cleaning products are poisonous and can burn skin; bending down to pick things up can cause painful back problems; dust can bring on coughing fits; wet floors are as slippery and as dangerous as an ice rink; and the lead snaking out from your vacuum cleaner – or any other electronic gadget designed to make life 'easier' – is a horrible trip hazard.

What's galling though is that, for all these dangers, a state of immaculate domestic perfection is all too fleeting. Children, pets and inconsiderate partners, will all conspire to mess things up and so force you to start all over again. Therefore, the easiest and by far the safest option is to stay in bed, pull the sheets over your head and forget all about keeping things spick and span.

One man who *definitely* came a cropper when tidying up was the landlord of The Old Cross Inn on Narrowgate in Alnwick. In 1725 or thereabouts, he made the mistake of tackling the front window of the pub. On the windowsill was a collection of discarded bottles, presumably left there after a night of hard drinking by locals. Unfortunately, while moving the bottles, the poor man dropped dead from a heart attack. His widow, fearing a curse, declared that the bottles should never be moved lest the same thing should happen again. Three centuries on, the pub has been renamed Dirty Bottles and has a thoroughly modern interior. The now dust-covered bottles remain in place, however, though kept safely out of reach behind glass. No matter how fastidious you may be, this is one cleaning task you really *don't* want to tackle. After all, why take the risk?

Address 32 Narrowgate, Alnwick, NE66 1JG, +44 (0)1665 606193, www.thedirtybottles.co.uk | **Getting there** Bus 473, X15 Max, X18 Max, 418 and various others to Alnwick Bus Station and then a short walk; parking at Greenwell Road (Part D) Car Park (requires parking disc available from Alnwick's Tourist Information Centre and some local shops) | **Hours** Sun–Fri noon–midnight, Sat noon–1am | **Tip** Barter Books is one of the largest second-hand bookshops in Europe and takes up the entirety of the former Alnwick railway station (www.barterbooks.co.uk).

7__Harry Hotspur Statue

He's one of our own

Henry Percy was destined for greatness – he was a Percy after all. Henry was the eldest son of Henry Percy, first Earl of Northumberland, and born at Alnwick Castle (see ch. 4) on 20 May, 1364. At the age of 12 he was knighted by King Edward III, along with two future kings: Richard II and Henry IV, both of whom would figure prominently in Henry's adult life.

Harry – no one refers to him as Henry – was well travelled. As a teen he accompanied the Earl of March to Ireland, and then later to Prussia. He also spent time in France on military campaigns, was sent to Cyprus on a diplomatic mission, and fought in Scotland with Richard II. It was the Scots, who in 1385, gave Harry the name Haatspore or Hotspur for the speed at which he and his men advanced into Scotland, and for his willingness to attack.

Richard did not benefit from his friendship with Harry. In cahoots with his father, Harry took part in a rebellion that saw Richard deposed in 1399 and Henry Bolingbroke crowned as King Henry IV. However, even that relationship soured, and the Percys rebelled again in 1403. Harry was killed at the Battle of Shrewsbury that year. Legend has it that, for all the bad blood between them, Henry wept upon seeing Harry's dead body.

Harry's legacy lived on long after his death. He plays an important role in Shakespeare's *Henry IV Part One*, before being killed by Henry in act five. Even though Harry is arguably the villain of the piece – he's on the 'wrong' side of history in opposing Henry, after all – he is at worst an anti-hero, courageous and noble, if hot-headed and quick to anger. Perhaps Harry's oddest legacy, though, is Tottenham Hotspur FC. The Percy family owned property on Tottenham Marshes, where – centuries later – the football club would make its home. The founders of the club thought Harry's fighting spirit was an ideal example for the players.

Address Pottergate, Alnwick, NE66 1JR | **Getting there** Bus 473, X15 Max, X18 Max, 418 and various others to Alnwick Bus Station and then a short walk; parking at Greenwell Road (Part D) Car Park (requires parking disc available from Alnwick's Tourist Information Centre and some local shops) | **Tip** Pottergate Tower, just a few minutes' walk from the Harry Hotspur Statue, was once part of Alnwick's medieval defences. It was rebuilt in a gothic style in the 18th century and is now let as holiday accommodation.

8 Lion Bridge

Roared bridge

The Lion Bridge over the River Aln has a certain something other bridges usually lack: a lion. He stands on all fours facing north, his mouth agape, and with his tail straight and curiously horizontal. He is the Percy Lion, the feline symbol of a noble family whose history is thoroughly entwined with that of Northumberland.

The House of Percy originated in Normandy at the manor of Percy-en-Auge. William de Percy arrived in England a few years after the invasion of 1066 by William the Conqueror. The first Percy estate was in Yorkshire and there the family remained until 1309, when Henry de Percy, First Baron Percy, purchased Alnwick Castle (see ch. 4). His eldest son – Henry, Second Baron Percy – supported King Edward III and gained further land and titles in Northumberland for his efforts. His son and grandson – both also Henrys – aided the English royal family too, with the younger Henry becoming the First Earl of Northumberland.

Other notable members of the family during the medieval period include Harry Hotspur; Henry Percy, Fourth Earl of Northumberland, who supported King Richard III, but whose army did not take part at the Battle of Bosworth Field, possibly leading to the defeat and death of Richard; and Algernon Percy, 10th Earl of Northumberland, who fought on the side of the Parliamentarians during the English Civil War, but who was opposed to the trial (and later execution) of King Charles I at the end of the war.

Ralph Percy, the 12th Duke of Northumberland, is the current owner of Alnwick Castle. The title was first created in 1551 for John Dudley, First Earl of Warwick. This did him no good at all as he was ultimately executed for high treason after supporting Lady Jane Grey as the rightful heir to the throne, rather than Queen Mary I. But that was the Percy way, sometimes on the winning side and sometimes not…

Address The Peth, Alnwick, Northumberland, NE66 2JX | Getting there Bus 473,
X15 Max, X18 Max, 418 and various others to Alnwick Bus Station and then a
10-minute walk; free car park on The Peth | Tip The Bakehouse Gallery showcases the
work of contemporary British artists and designers in what was the old town bakery
(www.bakehousegallery.com).

9 Poison Garden

Not to be taken internally

The first garden at Alnwick Castle was created in 1750 by Capability Brown for Hugh Percy, First Duke of Northumberland. This garden was then dug over to grow much-needed fruit and veg during World War II. After the war, financial restrictions saw the garden slowly decay into disrepair.

The new Alnwick Garden was the brainchild of Jane Percy, Duchess of Northumberland. Work began on its development in 1997, with the first phase completed in October 2001. The garden was then opened to the public and proved to be a hit. There are many singular attractions at Alnwick Garden, including the largest wooden treehouse in the world. However, arguably the most interesting feature – definitely the most deadly – is the Poison Garden, found behind a locked gate in its own walled-off space.

The Poison Garden is filled with roughly 100 different plant species, all of which are either toxic, narcotic or both. To avoid unnecessary death, the Poison Garden can only be visited under supervision on a guided tour. Touching, eating or even smelling the plants is a no-no for obvious reasons. In fact, so toxic are some of the plants that the gardeners need to wear protective clothing when tending to them.

Surprisingly, not all of the plants are particularly exotic. Many can be found growing in gardens across the UK. Take aconitum for example. It's an ornamental perennial with purple-blue flowers that resemble the cowls of monks, hence its common name of monkshood. Every part of the plant contains aconitine, an alkaloid that causes vomiting, diarrhoea or even cardiac arrest if swallowed. Agatha Christie used aconitum to despatch victims in two of her books: *4.50 from Paddington* and *They Do It with Mirrors*. Which is why you shouldn't argue with your nearest and dearest before making a visit to the Poison Garden…

THESE PLANTS CAN KILL

Address Denwick Lane, Alnwick, Northumberland, NE66 1YU, +44 (0)1665 511350, www.alnwickgarden.com | Getting there Bus 418 or X18 MAX to Allerburn Lea; paid parking at Alnwick Garden | Hours Apr–Oct daily 10am–5pm during term time, Apr–Oct daily 9am–6pm during Northumberland school holidays, reduced opening hours Nov–Mar (see website for details) | Tip Brizlee Tower is a wonderfully eccentric folly in Alnwick's Hulne Park, built in 1781 for Hugh Percy.

10 Tenantry Column

Sending the wrong message

An action can have unintended consequences. Need an example? Let's take a look at the Percy Tenantry Column, or the 'Farmers' Folly' as it's waggishly referred to locally. Next, we need to go back to 1816, the year after the Napoleonic Wars ended. The outbreak of peace was bad news for Northumbrian farmers, who'd benefitted financially from ever-increasing food prices during the wars. Now there was a depression and farmers were struggling.

Tenant farmers on land belonging to Hugh Percy, Second Duke of Northumberland, couldn't afford a rent increase. So they appealed to Percy's better nature to help them out. This worked out better than expected when Percy reduced their rents by a quarter. By the aristocratic standards of the time, this was an extremely magnanimous gesture. In gratitude, the tenants commissioned local architect David Stephenson to design a stone column in Percy's honour. And so, on 1 July, 1816, the foundation stone was laid, with the ceremony watched by a large crowd.

The completed column stands 83 feet tall, is topped by the Percy lion (with its horizontal tail pointing towards Scotland for no good reason), and has four lions arrayed around the base. On the western side of the base are carved the words *To Hugh, Duke of Northumberland K.G. This column is Erected, Dedicated and Inscribed By a Grateful and United Tenantry Anno Domini MDCCCXVI.*

So why the 'Farmers' Folly'? Percy, so the story goes, realising that his tenants weren't as hard up as they claimed, immediately increased their rents. Or did he? Sadly, it seems it's just a mischievous legend. Percy, who died on 10 July, 1817, never saw the completed column and it was presented to his son, Hugh Percy, Third Duke of Northumberland, instead. Can it therefore be used as an example of an unintended consequence? Probably not. But it really is a wonderful (lion's) tale.

Address Alnwick, Northumberland, NE66 2NP | Getting there Bus 418, X18 Max, X20 Max and 460 to Infirmary; parking at Greenwell Road (Part A) Car Park and then a short walk (requires parking disc available from Alnwick's Tourist Information Centre and some local shops) | Tip The Bailiffgate Museum & Gallery is a wonderful way to find out more about Alnwick and the surrounding area. The museum boasts permanent exhibits that uncover 10,000 years of history, as well as a gallery with a rolling programme of events (bailiffgatemuseum.co.uk).

11___*Flock Sphere*
Birds of feather…

The 'Bord Waalk' is a new £396,000 walking trail that starts at Hauxley Nature Reserve, curves around the coast to Amble, and from there takes you along the River Coquet to Warkworth. There will eventually be 12 sculptures dotted along the route, all inspired by the different types of bird that can be seen in the area. Not only that, but there will be a 'Bord Waalk' app with an augmented reality feature, related music, poetry, and information about the trail and the artists involved. Three of the sculptures along the route were in place by the end of 2022: *Tern Wings* by Jon Voss, *Bird Song* by Aether and Hemera, and *Flock Sphere* by Rob Mulholland.

Flock Sphere is a stainless-steel globe – approximately eight feet in diameter – into which bird shapes have been laser cut. A doorway has been created in the base so that it's possible to climb inside to view the sphere from within. From this perspective it's easy to imagine yourself as a bird, flying as a member of a flock. As Mulholland stated in his original proposal for *Flock Sphere*, it 'allows the viewer to consider their own relationship with natural world… specifically the relationship they have with the world of ornithology as they stand surrounded by the flock'.

Bird life along Northumberland's coast is varied, particularly during the summer months when migratory birds fly in to breed. The puffin is arguably the most charismatic of these migratory birds and can be seen nesting on the Farne Islands (see ch. 99), as well as Coquet Island just off the coast at Amble. The eider duck is equally characterful, and can be seen on the coast throughout the year. The eider duck was a favourite of St Cuthbert and for that reason they are known locally as cuddy ducks. The saint loved the ducks so much that he placed them under his protection. Monks who later ate or harmed the ducks in any way were allegedly struck down by 'Cuthbert's Curse', and one was even said to have died.

Address The Braid, Amble, Northumberland, NE65 0WU, www.theambler.co.uk | Getting there Bus X20 Max to Fourways and then an 11-minute walk; free parking at Amble Braid Car Park | Tip Originally an open-cast mine, the thoroughly naturalised Hauxley Nature Reserve is a great place to see a wide variety of birds, as well as stoats, red squirrels and otters (www.nwt.org.uk).

12 Town Square

From shore to ship and back again

In Amble Town Square can be found a stone onto which has been carved a wonderfully semi-abstract design and a single word: Mauretania. This commemorates RMS *Mauretania*, an ocean liner built on Tyneside for Cunard by Wigham Richardson and Swan Hunter, and launched in 1906.

Mauretania was the world's largest ship when she first entered service, a record quickly broken by RMS *Olympic*. On her maiden voyage in 1907 she was awarded the Blue Riband for the fastest eastbound crossing of the Atlantic. She then won the westbound Blue Riband in 1909, holding on to both records for 20 years. Speed was an asset when she was pressed into military service at the outbreak of World War I. Troops who sailed on her to Gallipoli, and then later from Canada, must have been grateful that attacks by prowling U-boats were less likely to be successful.

Mauretania was fast, thanks to her state-of-the-art steam turbine power plants, invented by engineer Charles Parsons in 1884. *Turbinia*, the first ship powered by a steam turbine, demonstrated their potential by outrunning every other vessel at a naval review on 26 June, 1897. Cheekily, this was an unannounced appearance and was watched – perhaps with some amusement – by Queen Victoria, who was then celebrating her Diamond Jubilee.

On 6 July, 1935, *Mauretania* was on her final voyage, sailing along the Northumbrian coast to Rosyth, to be broken up. At 10.25am, the clerk to Amble Urban Council sent a cheery message to the captain of the *Mauretania*, Arthur Tillotson Brown. It read: 'Amble to *Mauretania*. Greetings from Amble, last port in England, to still the finest ship on the seas.' An equally cheery message was sent back: 'To the last and kindliest port in England, greetings and thanks. *Mauretania*.' And so, since that day, Amble has been known (with a slight change in wording) as 'the friendliest port'.

Address Amble, Northumberland, NE65 0DN | Getting there Bus X 20 Max to Four ways; four hours' free parking at Amble Town Centre Car Park | Tip Artefacts rescued from the *Mauretania*, as well as *Turbinia* herself, are on display in the Discovery Museum in Newcastle (www.discoverymuseum.org.uk).

13 __ Jack Charlton Statue
Football legend

Ashington punches above its weight when it comes to producing sporting heroes. Katherine Copeland, Olympic Gold Medal winning rower, is from the town. As is Steve Harrison, former first-class cricketer. But perhaps the greatest were three footballers: Jackie Milburn, Bobby Charlton and his older brother, Jack Charlton. On 29 October, 2022 a statue of the latter was unveiled in Hirst Park in Ashington.

Jack Charlton was born on 8 May, 1935 into a mining family. He learned to love football thanks to his mother, Cissie (a Milburn and cousin of Jackie). Cissie played football in the street with her four boys (the two youngest, Gordon and Tommy never played football professionally). However, Cissie was slightly dismissive of Jack's talents. Possibly for that reason he turned down the offer to play a trial for Leeds United when he was 15. After leaving school and spending a miserable year working in one of Ashington's mines, Jack was approached by Leeds again. This time he didn't hesitate.

A gangly six foot three inches, Jack made his debut for Leeds in 1953. However, his career was interrupted by National Service, when he spent two years serving in the Household Cavalry. Jack returned to Leeds in 1955 with a new-found confidence as a player. By all accounts, this self-assurance occasionally tipped over into arrogance. In 1961, Don Revie was hired as manager of Leeds. Revie saw potential in Jack and pushed him to mature as a player.

The reward was a place – with Bobby – on the England team that won the 1966 World Cup. Jack stayed with Leeds until retiring in 1973. He went on to manage Middlesbrough, Sheffield Wednesday and Newcastle United, and was the much-loved manager of Ireland's national team for nine years. Jack retired to Northumberland and spent much of his time fishing. He died on 10 July, 2020. Douglas Jennings' statue is a fitting tribute to one of the greats.

Address Hirst Park, Ashington, Northumberland, NE63 9FX, www.northumberland.gov.uk |
Getting there Bus 35 to Hirst Park; parking at Hirst Park | Hours Daily 8.30am–dusk | Tip
St James' Park is the home of Newcastle United, a team Charlton managed in 1985. See the
grounds from an unusual angle by taking one of the regular rooftop tours (www.nufc.co.uk).

14 Pitmen Painters

Underground art movement

Coal mining was a brutal and often dangerous job. In *The Road to Wigan Pier*, George Orwell famously compared a mine to hell, describing the 'heat, noise, confusion, darkness, foul air, and, above all, unbearably cramped space'. He also observed that 'You could quite easily drive a car right across the north of England and never once remember that hundreds of feet below the road you are on the miners are hacking at the coal.'

Orwell creates a compelling and vivid snapshot of life as a miner, but he did not – could not – tell the entire story. A richer, more human tale is told in the Ashington Group Gallery in the Woodhorn Museum. The group developed out of the Ashington branch of the Workers' Education Association, formed in the late 1920s. In 1934, the WEA and Durham University arranged for Robert Lyon, an artist and teacher, to run an art appreciation class for Ashington's miners. The men were encouraged by Lyon to create their own paintings, using their domestic life, their work, and their surroundings as subjects. This they did for the next 50 years.

The Ashington Group – also known as the Pitmen Painters – met weekly in a hut they rented for the purpose. Their first exhibition was held at the Hatton Gallery in Newcastle in 1936, followed by another – entitled 'Unprofessional Painting' – in Gateshead. Their work was also shown in London in 1939, and later was praised by prominent artists of the time, such as Henry Moore.

The group had a lower profile post-war, though they continued to meet every week, to paint and talk about art. When the group's hut was demolished in 1983, Oliver Kilbourn – a founding member – had the group's paintings put into trust. It is these paintings that are now displayed at Woodhorn. Another legacy of the Ashington Group was *The Pitmen Painters*, a 2007 play by Lee Hall that was a hit both in the UK and on Broadway.

51

54

52

55

Address Woodhorn Museum, Queen Elizabeth II Country Park, Ashington, Northumberland, NE63 9YF, +44 (0)1670 624455, museumsnorthumberland.org.uk | **Getting there** Bus 1, X20 MAX and X21 Sapphire to Woodhorn Villas and then a 25-minute walk; free parking at Woodhorn Museum | **Hours** Wed–Sun 10am–4pm | **Tip** The library in the Mining Institute boasts one of the largest collections of books on mining and associated engineering in the world (www.mininginstitute.org.uk).

15 Bamburgh Castle
Family home

There has been a fortification of some sort on the site of Bamburgh Castle since the sixth century. The Kings of Northumbria lived in a forerunner of Bamburgh Castle, though in a structure made of wood rather than stone. Oswald, the most influential of these monarchs, was the man who invited Aidan to Northumbria and thus brought Christianity to the region. Bamburgh Castle is also linked to the legend of King Arthur, described by Thomas Malory in *Le Morte d'Arthur* as the site of Joyous Gard, home of the heroic Sir Lancelot.

Bamburgh Castle sits on an impressively steep and craggy outcrop of the Whin Sill formation. However, this lofty elevation didn't prevent the sacking of an earlier castle during a Viking raid in 993. After the Norman invasion, the new overlords rebuilt the castle. The oldest part still standing is the keep or Great Tower. It was built in 1164 and used as a garrison for English soldiers, who fought in the various bad-tempered border conflicts with the Scottish. Ironically, the castle suffered its greatest damage during the War of the Roses, a purely English affair. A Lancastrian stronghold, it was successfully attacked by Yorkist forces in 1464, who made use of new-fangled cannon. The castle has the dubious honour of being the first English castle conquered through the use of artillery.

By the 18th century, the castle was in a dilapidated state. In 1704 it was sold to Lord Crewe. A trust was then set up to maintain the building after his death in 1721. Under the stewardship of Dr John Sharp, the keep and court rooms were repaired, and a hospital established within castle grounds. Fittingly, a portrait of Sharp – who effectively created a proto-welfare state in Bamburgh – hangs in the King's Hall. The castle was then extensively refurbished by the industrialist William Armstrong, who bought it in 1894. The Armstrong family still live there to this day.

Address Links Road, Bamburgh, Northumberland, NE69 7DF, +44 (0)1668 214208, www.bamburghcastle.com | **Getting there** Bus 418 or X18 Max to Lord Crewe Hotel; very limited on-street parking on Front Street or paid parking at the Links Road Car Park | **Hours** Daily 10am–4pm | **Tip** Prudhoe Castle – an hour's drive south west from Bamburgh – uniquely resisted Scottish siege during the medieval period (www.english-heritage.org.uk).

16 Grace Darling Memorial

Pay tribute to a local heroine

On 5 September, 1838, the steamship *Forfarshire* began her journey north from Hull, bound for Dundee. She was laden with cargo and roughly 40 passengers, the number imprecise as no passenger list was drawn up. Also on board were 22 crew members, her captain, John Humble, and his wife. Trouble began that night when, in heavy seas, one of the boilers sprang a leak. Despite an attempt at repair, the problem continued.

That evening – partly under sail – the *Forfarshire* neared Berwick-upon-Tweed. And then gale-force winds blew in from the north. The stress on the ship caused the boilers to fail and she began to drift south, pushed back by the storm. Humble decided to make for the Farne Islands (see ch. 99) but the high seas made navigation difficult. At 4am on the morning of the 7th, the *Forfarshire* struck Big Harcar Rock, one mile from Longstone Lighthouse.

Grace Darling was the daughter of William Darling, the keeper at Longstone. Unable to sleep, Grace saw a dark shape off Harcar Rock. Waking her father, they studied the sight through a telescope and thought it must be a shipwreck. By daylight they could see movement on the rock. With the storm still raging, William knew that the lifeboat at Seahouses could not put to sea. And so, at Grace's instigation, the pair set off in their coble. With Grace rowing, William skilfully navigated their way to the wreck. Once there, the pair found nine survivors, too many for their small boat; two trips would be necessary. Helped by two crew members, the coble was rowed back to Longstone carrying three of the other survivors. The last four were rescued less than an hour later.

The bravery of Grace that morning was a contemporary sensation. Sadly, she died just four years later of tuberculosis aged 26. Fittingly, her canopied memorial in St Aidan's churchyard is visible to sailors passing the Bamburgh coastline.

Address St Aidan's Church, Radcliffe Road, Bamburgh, Northumberland, NE69 7AB |
Getting there Bus 418 or X18 Max to The Grove or Church Street; very limited on-street
parking on Front Street or paid parking at the Links Road Car Park and then a 10-minute
walk | **Tip** The RNLI Grace Darling Museum tells the story of the *Forfarshire* and Grace's
role in the rescue of survivors. On display are objects that belonged to Grace and her family,
as well as the coble – a Northumbrian rowing boat – used in the rescue (rnli.org).

17 Spindlestone Heughs
Slippery customer

Long, long ago, the beloved wife of the elderly King of Bamburgh passed away. The king was inconsolable, for he loved his queen with all his heart. Only his pretty daughter, the gracious Princess Margaret, remained to comfort him, for Childe Wynd, his dashing son, had been far from the kingdom for many a year, on a quest for fame and fortune.

One day, a beautiful but black-hearted witch arrived at the castle of the king. Using dark magic, she beguiled and seduced him and within weeks they were married. However, the new queen was jealous of Princess Margaret, for the maiden was a favourite with the young knights of her father's court. Plotting mischief, the witch cast a spell over Margaret, who, come the morning, found herself transformed into a hideous dragon. Only the return of Childe Wynd, whom many feared dead, would break the curse. Poor Princess Margaret. Terrified of what she had become, she slithered and crawled out of the castle to seek shelter in a cave in Spindlestone Heughs. Only hunger drove her back out into the countryside, where she fed on the sheep and cattle of nearby farms.

Months passed. In that time, word reached Childe Wynd of the 'Laidley Worm' that terrorised his father's kingdom. After a year and a day of sailing, Childe Wynd faced the dragon. Sword in hand and grim of face, Childe Wynd rushed at the creature. However, before the fatal blow could be struck, he heard a quiet but brave voice requesting mercy. Childe Wynd lowered his sword, his heart filled with love for the beast. Bowing, he kissed it gently on the forehead. The dragon returned to its cave to emerge once more as the Princess Margaret. Hearing the news that her spell was broken, the wicked queen attempted to flee. Soon captured, she turned into a warty toad, doomed to spend the rest of her life spitting venom at any pretty maid who dared to cross her path.

Address Waren Mill, Northumberland, NE70 7EE | Getting there Free parking at Budle Bay and then a 30-minute walk | Tip The crags of Spindlestone Heugh are on the route of a public footpath. Look out for the natural stone column known as Bridle Rock, over which Childe Wynd allegedly threw his horse's bridle before tackling the dragon.

18 — William Beveridge's Grave
Slaying giants

Within the boundaries of the parish of Bavington is one of North-umberland's oldest churches. St Aidan's, in the hamlet of Thockring-ton, was built in the 12th century for the de Umfraville family. It is also the last resting place of William Beveridge, who helped pave the way for Britain's welfare state.

Beveridge was born in Rangpur on 5 March, 1879. In 1897, he went up to Balliol College, Oxford, where a life-long interest in social reform developed. In 1902, after graduation, Beveridge accepted the post of sub-warden of Toynbee Hall. It was there that he met Sidney and Beatrice Webb, members of the socialist Fabian Society. The Webbs had a profound influence on Beveridge, and helped to shape his belief in the need for the likes of unemployment relief and old age pensions. It was also through the Webbs that Beveridge met Winston Churchill in 1907.

Churchill was then a member of the ruling Liberal Party. Working as a civil servant in the Board of Trade, Beveridge helped draw up forward-looking legislation such as the Labour Exchanges Act of 1909 and the 1911 National Insurance Act. After World War I, Beveridge returned to academic life, first as Director of the LSE and then as master of University College, Oxford.

In December 1940, Beveridge was invited to chair a government committee to investigate social provision in Britain and make suggestions for change. The 'Social Insurance and Allied Services' report was published in 1942 and was an immediate sensation with the public. It outlined the need to slay the 'five giants' of idleness, ignorance, disease, squalor and want, through the provision of universal social insurance and health care. Ironically, Churchill was unimpressed, but when the Labour Party were elected to power in 1945, Beveridge's plans were put into action with the creation of the NHS and the cradle-to-grave welfare state.

WILLIAM HENRY
LORD BEVERIDGE
of Tuggal
5 March 1879
16 March 1963.

Address Thockrington, Northumberland, NE48 4DH | Getting there Very limited off-road parking and then a walk uphill across rough grassland | Tip The grave of Connie Leathart can also be found in the churchyard of St Aidan's. Leathart was a pioneering female pilot who flew fighter and bomber aircraft for the Air Transport Auxiliary during World War II.

19__Beadnell Harbour
Go West, young man…

You have to admire a place that bucks the trend and does things differently. Many coastal communities in Northumberland have a harbour. However, only the village of Beadnell has a harbour that faces west, quite an achievement when the sea is very definitely to the east. It is in fact the only harbour on the east coast of England to pull off this rather neat trick.

The harbour was built in the 18th century and then improved and enlarged for John Wood in 1798. Wood was a local landowner and the owner of Beadnell Hall. His estate contained substantial outcrops of limestone and deposits of coal, both of which were valuable commodities. Wood also had a limekiln built on the harbour to calcinate his limestone to produce calcium oxide (or quicklime). This very dangerous and unstable compound has a number of applications, including the preparation of whitewash, and as a fertiliser for acidic soils. It was also once used to cover dead bodies as it helped mask the smell of decomposition.

So lucrative was the trade in quicklime that Wood had two further kilns built sooner after the first. The three kilns were not used for their original purpose for long, however. By 1822 they were repurposed to cure herring, a fish that was once caught in huge numbers off the coast of Northumberland. Now, local fishermen use the impressively substantial kilns purely for storage.

The beach at Beadnell was once used for horse racing. The first race meeting was held in March 1667. The event entered the records thanks to a letter written by a jockey from Ellingham on the 17th of that month. It was a note requesting that his mistress, a Mrs Haggerston, obtain permission from his master 'to let him ride Laurence Gibson's galloper at Bedenel Races'. The last race (to date at least) was held on 26 April, 1827, when IOU won the Three Mile Plate for his (or her) owner, Mr Boag.

Address Harbour Road, Beadnell, Northumberland, NE67 5BH | **Getting there** Bus 418 to The Haven and then a 13-minute walk; paid parking at Beadnell Bay Car Park | **Tip** The Salt Water Café offers a range of hearty breakfasts, as well as a lunch and dinner menu with a seafood slant (www.saltwatercafe.co.uk).

20 Bedlington Terrier
Good doggie!

Northern Britain has the curious knack of producing breeds of terrier. There's the Yorkshire Terrier, the West Highland, the Airedale, and the Border. In the 1820s, Joseph Ainsley successfully produced a new type of terrier, which was fittingly named after his home town of Bedlington. (It's probable that the breed originated earlier than this – possibly bred by gypsies who lived in the town – but it's Ainsley who generally gets the credit.)

Bedlington was a colliery town during the 19th and early 20th centuries. Miners loved the Bedlington Terrier. According to Rawdon B. Lee's incredibly comprehensive book *A History and Description of the Modern Dogs of Great Britain and Ireland (The Terriers)*, the pitmen 'trained the best specimens, and would not dispose of them for "untold gold"'. What's slightly odd about this is that, at first glance, Bedlingtons don't act or look like dogs owned by hardened men of industry. They're gentle in nature and good with children, have appealing round faces, and sport a natty woolly coat that makes them look more like lambs than dogs. They are, however, tenacious and fearless hunting dogs and were used by miners to catch rats down in the pits, as well as more generally to kill badgers and foxes. They're also excellent swimmers and positively love playing in snow.

The National Bedlington Terrier Club of England was formed in 1877, and 21 years later the breed was registered with the Kennel Club of England. The appeal of the Bedlington Terrier has crossed the Atlantic too. In 1948, a Bedlington called Rock Ridge Night Rocket won Best in Show at the Westminster Kennel Club Dog Show in New York. Today, the breed is rightly celebrated in Bedlington. Metal likenesses of the terrier welcome visitors to the town, and charming depictions of the dog are used ornamentally on park benches – though strangely not the lampposts…

Address Bedlington, Northumberland, NE22 | Getting there Bus 2, 19, 43 Sapphire, X 21 Sapphire or X 22 Sapphire to Front Street West; free parking for two hours at Schalksmuhle Road Car Park | Tip Plessey Woods Country Park offers pleasant woodland and riverside walking for everyone, including dogs and their owners (www.northumberland.gov.uk).

21__Chinese Gingall
Spoils of war

A small cannon is on public display in Bellingham, just a short walk from the Town Hall. It has stood in its present spot for nearly 100 years, keeping the neighbouring Manchester Square safe. Unlike a sturdy medieval cannon, it has an appealing slim – almost delicate – appearance.

The cannon is a Chinese gingall and was presented to the town by Sir Edward Charlton. It was captured on 17 June, 1900 by British sailors serving on HMS *Orlando* during the Boxer Rebellion. A gingall was essentially a large gun that fired iron bullets, mounted on a wooden frame. Though relatively clumsy compared with a pistol or rifle, gingalls could be a devastatingly effective weapon. In 1860, the *London Gazette* printed a list of British servicemen injured by gingalls, including details such as a 'contusion of right shoulder by large gingall ball', 'gingall ball through right thigh', and the eye-watering 'gingall ball, thigh and testicle'.

The Boxer Rebellion was a violent uprising in China with the aim of ridding the country of foreigners, Western Christian missionaries in particular. 'Boxer' was the name given to a Chinese secret society involved in the uprising: the Righteous and Harmonious Fists (*Yìhéquán*). The Boxers practised a form of martial art that they believed would make them invulnerable to bullets. In this they were mistaken. The rebellion was brutally suppressed by the armies of the Eight Nation Alliance, and ended when Peking (now Beijing) was captured in August 1900. After the signing of the 'Boxer Protocol', China was forced to pay reparations to the victors.

Sir Edward Charlton served with distinction in the Royal Navy, eventually rising to the rank of admiral. He served in the Anglo-Egyptian war of 1882 as well as in World War I. Strangely, Charlton wasn't involved in the Boxer Rebellion, so how or where he acquired the gingall is something of a mystery.

Address Bellingham, Northumberland, NE48 2AS | **Getting there** Bus 680 Tynedale Links to The Practice or to Parkside Place; limited free parking off B 6320 in Bellingham | **Tip** Learn more about the fascinating history of Bellingham and surrounding area at The Heritage Centre (bellingham-heritage.org.uk).

22 Hareshaw Linn

Nature trumps industry

The verdant countryside around Bellingham was once an industrial landscape, exploited for the underlying ironstone. This iron-rich rock was first heated in roasting kilns to remove impurities. Local deposits of coal provided the fuel for the kilns, as well as providing coke for Bellingham's two blast furnaces. The furnaces were used to create pig iron for use across Northumberland; Bellingham iron was used in the construction of the High Level Bridge in Newcastle, for instance. However, the works, established in 1833, were demolished after a short 15 years of operation. The lack of a railway connection ultimately made them economically unviable.

Take the Hareshaw Linn path from Bellingham and you'll see one relic of the town's industrial past: Hareshaw Low Dam. The dam was built to supply water to the ironworks and was surplus to requirements when industrial activity ceased. It was repaired in 2004 and is now a Scheduled Ancient Monument.

Further on from the dam, the path takes you into deciduous woodland. The woodland – a mix of elm, hazel and oak – is a Site of Special Scientific Interest. Over 50 species of lichen are found there, as well as varieties of mosses, ferns and liverworts. The wood is also home to numerous species of animals, including birds such as wood warbler and spotted flycatcher, as well as red squirrel and badger. There are also fairies, who live near a 'fairy spring'. (Note: seeing fairies on the walk is *not* guaranteed.)

The path crosses over the Hareshaw Burn six times to end at Hareshaw Linn. Although not the highest waterfall in the region, Hareshaw Linn is arguably the most aesthetically pleasing. In an amphitheatre of sandstone, the 30-foot waterfall fans out across the rock face so that the cascade is far wider at the bottom than at the top. It's utterly enchanting, and where the cares and worries of the modern world can be forgotten for an hour or two.

Address Armstrong Square, Bellingham, Northumberland, NE48 2BZ, www.northumberlandnationalpark.org.uk | **Getting there** Bus 680 Tynedale Links to The Practice or to Parkside Place and then a 35-minute walk; free parking at the Hareshaw Linn Car Park and then a 30-minute walk | **Tip** The Battlesteads Dark Sky Observatory offers a range of talks, courses and stargazing activities for those interested in astronomy or who want to find out more about observing the night sky (www.battlesteads.com/observatory).

23 — The Lang Pack

Grave error

In the grounds of St Cuthbert's Church in Bellingham is a peculiar rectangular gravestone, known as The Lang Pack. Beneath it lies the body of a villain who was killed during an audacious robbery some 300 years ago. The tale as told goes something like this…

It is the end of a bitterly cold winter's day in 1723. Colonel Ridley, the owner of Lee Hall on the banks of the River North Tyne near Redesmouth, is away in London. The house is in the care of three servants, Alice, Richard and Edward, who are under strict instructions not to allow anyone into the house. They are, therefore, thoroughly disconcerted when there is a knock at the door. The door is cautiously opened to reveal a pedlar. He begs to be allowed to come in and stay the night, but the three, mindful of their master's instructions, refuse the request. The pedlar wheedles and whines to no avail. They do, however, agree to look after the pedlar's large pack while he seeks lodgings elsewhere.

A few hours later all is quiet at Lee Hall and everyone is in bed except for Alice. Passing the pack in the hallway, she is startled to see it move. Terrified, she runs to fetch Richard and Edward. The latter, armed with his master's blunderbuss, shoots at the pack. With a groan, out falls a man, fatally wounded and breathing his last. On a chain around the man's neck hangs a silver whistle. The three quickly realise that the man is part of plot to rob the house, the whistle to summon his accomplices while they slept.

Help is sought from neighbours and, once a well-armed group is assembled at Lee Hall, the whistle blown. From the dark come a gang on horseback. Four are immediately shot and killed by the defenders; the rest flee in panic. Come daylight and the bodies have vanished, never to be found. The body of the man in the pack is eventually buried at St Cuthbert's, his identity a mystery that may never be solved.

Address Bellingham, Northumberland, NE48 2JP | Getting there Bus 680 Tynedale Links to The Practice or to Parkside Place; limited free parking off B 6320 in Bellingham | Tip The neighbouring Town Hall is a delightful Victorian building built in the Gothic Revival style. In 1964, the Newcastle-based pop group The Animals debuted 'The House of the Rising Sun' during a performance at the town hall. The single version of the song was a huge hit for the band in both the UK and USA.

24 Elizabethan Walls
Who does Berwick belong to?

Berwick suffered a tug-of-war between England and Scotland for centuries. It was Scottish in the 11th century, English in the late 12th, and then sold back to Scotland by King Richard I to fund his Crusade. That didn't settle the matter. Ownership of Berwick was bitterly contested until 1482 when the English crown took and held on to the town. The town has been English ever since.

This history of often hotly contested ownership does mean that Berwick has something no other town in Britain has: a complete set of defensive walls. They were built in 1558 to deter the Scots from taking possession of Berwick once again. The walls are roughly a mile and a quarter long, with four gates that allow entry into the town. They were built in an Italianate style, with five large bastions. These project out from the curtain wall and would have made it easy for defenders to protect the entire wall with gunfire.

Curiously, although Berwick was an English possession from 1482, it was 'of the kingdom, but not in it'. Any official document – such as a new law or Royal Proclamation – had to include Berwick, otherwise the terms of that document didn't apply to the town. This anomaly wasn't rectified until the Wales and Berwick Act of 1746, which stated that any act of Parliament would 'henceforth be deemed and taken to comprehend and include the Dominion of Wales and Town of Berwick-upon-Tweed'.

Despite this legal tidying up, some claim that Berwick was once at war with Russia for nearly 60 years. In 1854, Queen Victoria signed a declaration of war with Russia as 'Queen of Great Britain, Ireland, Berwick-upon-Tweed and the British Dominions beyond the sea'. In 1856 she then carelessly forgot to mention Berwick in the peace treaty. The discrepancy was not discovered until 1914 when a separate treaty between Russia and Berwick was finally signed. Sadly, this is not true and is just a weirdly tenacious myth.

Address Berwick-upon-Tweed, Northumberland, TD15 1HN | Getting there Bus 32, 34, 60, 67, 236, X 15 MAX, X 18 MAX and various others to Golden Square; train to Berwick Railway Station and then a short walk; free parking at Parade Car Park for two hours (requires parking disc available from shops in Berwick) | Tip The Elizabethan walls were preceded by a medieval castle overlooking the River Tweed and viewable from the riverside path (www.english-heritage.org.uk).

25 Gunpowder Magazine
Trying not to raise the roof

Some everyday items are strangely dangerous. In 1981 there was a fire at the General Foods factory in Banbury, Oxfordshire. It was caused when a large cloud of custard powder ignited, causing an explosion that damaged the building and injured nine people (but fortunately caused no fatalities). Slightly bizarrely, the water from the fire engines used to put out the fire created vast quantities of custard, which then poured out on to the street. Berwick doesn't have a custard factory, but it does have a building that once stored an even more dangerous powder: the Gunpowder Magazine.

The mid-18th century was an unsettled time. On 21 September, 1745, Charles Stuart and his Jacobite army won the Battle of Prestonpans in East Lothian. An invasion of England was the obvious next move by the rebels, with Berwick the most likely route into the country. Unfortunately, Berwick was less ready than it thought. The town *did* have a large store of gunpowder, kept in the Brass Bastion built into the Elizabethan Walls (see ch. 24). However, it was found to be damp and therefore completely useless.

The Jacobite Rebellion of 1745 ultimately failed and Berwick was never attacked. Nevertheless, the fear of another uprising remained. And so the Gunpowder Magazine was built in 1751, a dry and above all safe place to house explosives. This was achieved through some cunning design. Surrounded by a high stone wall, the magazine has no windows. Instead, there are eight external buttresses, four on each side of the two longest walls. These buttresses were added so that an explosion would be directed upwards, rather than outwards. Inside, the barrels of gunpowder were kept off the floor on wooden racks. Candles were understandably forbidden and soldiers were required to wear special clothing to prevent accidental sparks: boot with nails in the soles were banned. Thankfully, these safety features were never put to the test. And no-one ever desserted their post either.

Address The Walls, Berwick-upon-Tweed, Northumberland, TD15 1JG, www.english-heritage.org.uk | Getting there Bus 235 or Hoppa to Marygate and then an short walk; train to Berwick Railway Station and then a 15-minute walk; free parking at Parade Car Park for two hours (requires parking disc available from shops in Berwick) and then a short walk | Hours Viewable from the outside only except on occasional open days | Tip Berwick Barracks was built in the early 18th century to house soldiers ready to combat Jacobite uprisings (www.english-heritage.org.uk).

26 Lions House

'I'm sure he once walked down our street'

One of the quirkier number-one hits of 1978 was Brian and Michael's 'Matchstalk Men and Matchstalk Cats and Dogs'. The song paid tribute to the artist Laurence Stephen Lowry, who had died just two years previously. Asked in 2013 why he wrote the song, Michael Colemen said simply, 'I've always loved Lowry and his paintings. It was an affection more than knowing anything about art, really.' Coleman is far from alone in loving Lowry. He is arguably the most well known of Britain's 20th-century painters, with souvenirs and prints of his work still best sellers.

Lowry was a keen amateur painter, and in 1915 attended evening classes at Salford School of Art. Lowry was inspired by the industrial scenes of his home town, recording both the beauty and the ugliness of the mills and factories of the area. He was also a keen painter of people going about their lives on the streets of Salford, captured for posterity in his deceptively simple, but highly original and distinctive style.

Salford was not the only town Lowry took inspiration from, however – he took a real shine to Berwick-upon-Tweed, too. Lowry frequently spent his holidays in the town, creating more than 30 paintings and drawings over the course of 40 years. In 2009, one of his paintings, *A Market Place, Berwick-upon-Tweed*, sold for £541,250 at auction. Lowry was so taken with Berwick that, in 1947, he contemplated buying 'The Lions', a splendid Georgian house overlooking the coast. He was ultimately dissuaded when an architect friend declared that it was 'rampant with damp'. After this, the house stood derelict for a number of years and by 1971 was under threat of demolition. Fortunately, in 1976 (coincidentally the year Lowry died), it was bought by the Berwick-upon-Tweed Preservation Trust and restored. It is now holiday accommodation, perfect for budding artists or those who appreciate a fine sea view.

Address The Walls, Berwick-upon-Tweed, Northumberland, TD15 1JG | Getting there Bus 235 or Hoppa to Marygate and then a short walk; train to Berwick Railway Station and then a 15-minute walk; free parking at Parade Car Park for two hours (requires parking disc available from shops in Berwick) and then a short walk | Hours Viewable from the outside only, although you can book it through crabtreeandcrabtree.com | Tip The Lowry Trail in Berwick is a short self-guided walk around parts of Berwick-upon-Tweed that Lowry was familiar with and painted. Panels along the route reproduce relevant paintings with a short but informative description of the area (starts on Dewar's Lane, Berwick-upon-Tweed).

27 Royal Border Bridge
'It's deep water, that's why a duck'

The approach to Berwick-upon-Tweed railway station is a particular highlight when travelling by train between Newcastle and Edinburgh. For that is when you cross over the River Tweed atop the splendid Royal Border Bridge. Look east from the bridge and you'll see the attractive town of Berwick, the river and its road bridges, and the North Sea glittering in the far distance.

You can see so much because the train is 126 feet above the river. And that's not the only impressive statistic, either. The bridge is 2,160 feet long in total, and 8 million cubic feet of stone and 2.5 million bricks were used in its construction. There are 28 arches along its length, 13 of which span the Tweed. Don't worry though, there is absolutely no danger of the bridge sinking into the mud. The foundations are 40 feet deep and stand on solid bedrock.

The Royal Border Bridge was designed by Robert Stephenson, son of railway pioneer George Stephenson, and who was also responsible for the equally vertiginous (and contemporary) High Level Bridge in Newcastle. The foundation stone for the 'Tweed Viaduct' – as it was initially referred to – was laid on 15 May, 1847. Construction was remarkably speedy given the scale of the project. On 29 August, 1850, the Royal Border Bridge was officially opened by Queen Victoria and Prince Albert.

The bridge connected the Edinburgh to Berwick line, owned by North British Railway, to the Tweedmouth to Newcastle line, owned by Newcastle & Berwick Railway. The opening of the bridge must have been a huge relief for passengers travelling between England and Scotland (and vice versa). Before 1848 – when a temporary wooden railway bridge was built – a horse-drawn carriage was used to ferry passengers (and their luggage, presumably) between the stations at Tweedmouth and Berwick. All you have to do now is sit back, relax and enjoy the view.

Address Royal Border Bridge Viewpoint, Tweedmouth, Berwick-upon-Tweed, Northumberland, TD15 2HJ | **Getting there** Bus Hoppa to West End Place and then a short walk; train to Berwick Railway Station and then a 20-minute walk; free parking near the Royal Border Bridge Viewpoint | **Tip** Berwick's Old Bridge – a road and pedestrian bridge – was completed in 1621 and is the oldest bridge over the River Tweed in Berwick.

28 Lord Crewe Arms
Spirits available

The Lord Crewe Arms is a hotel and pub in the charming and pictur-esque village of Blanchland. The building dates from the 12th century and was originally used as a lodge and guest house by the abbots of Blanchland Abbey. In 1539, after the dissolution of the monasteries, the abbey land and buildings were sold off. Then, in 1704, the Bishop of Durham, Lord Nathaniel Crewe, acquired Blanchland. This was through his marriage to Dorothy Forster, whose family had previ-ously owned Blanchland, as well as Bamburgh Castle, which Crewe also took possession of (see ch. 15).

Curiously, after that fateful year the Lord Crewe Arms slowly gained a reputation for being haunted. One alleged spectral visitor is a monk dressed in a white cassock. For some reason he is only ever seen in the Radcliffe guest room, where he likes to rearrange the furniture. He was last seen by an American tourist in the 1990s, standing silently at the end of the bed until fading peacefully away. Who the monk was and why he only haunts one particular room is a complete mystery. Equally puzzling are the reports of a group of black-clad monks occasionally seen in the garden, accompanied by the pealing of a long-gone abbey bell.

Another ghost is that of Dorothy Forster (confusingly, not Crewe's wife, but her niece). Her brother Tom was a Jacobite supporter, who was made a general during the rebellion of 1715. Unsuited to com-mand, he surrendered at the Battle of Preston. Tom was taken to London and imprisoned in Newgate Prison accused of high treason, the penalty for which was public execution. Fortunately, Dorothy was wily and courageous. She engineered Tom's escape from New-gate in April 1716 and smuggled him onto a boat bound for France. Dorothy lived in the Lord Crewe Arms until her death. Ever since, her spirit implores visitors to deliver a letter to Tom to tell him that it is finally safe to return home.

Address The Square, Blanchland, Northumberland, DH8 9SP, +44 (0)1434 677100, www.lordcrewearmsblanchland.co.uk | Getting there Bus 773 to Lord Crewe Arms or Clap Shaw; free parking in Blanchland Car Park | Tip The White Monk Refectory & Tearoom offers a wide range of freshly cooked food and drink in an atmospheric setting.

29 Shildon Engine House
Rural industry

It's hard now to appreciate how industrialised the North Pennines once were. The moors of Northumberland and County Durham once thrummed with the sounds of mining and steam-powered machinery. Only a few scattered and ruined remnants now remain to remind of us of those times. One spectacular example can be found just a few minutes' drive from the village of Blanchland.

As the name suggests, the Shildon Engine House once housed a steam engine, which was used to pump water from the nearby Easterby Hall and Company lead mine. The engine was built in 1808 by Boulton and Watt, an engineering firm based in Birmingham. The company was a partnership between Matthew Boulton and James Watt, with Watt supplying the engineering know-how. Delivering the engine to a remote location like Blanchland was time-consuming and difficult, which perhaps should have been a warning to Easterby Hall. The steam engine required huge quantities of coal, which also had to be brought in from elsewhere. The sheer cost of maintaining a steady supply of coal made the engine uneconomical. Although records are scant, it's highly probable that it was in use for less than a decade. The engine was eventually sold and installed at the Walker Colliery in Newcastle upon Tyne.

The building survived and in 1861 was converted into housing. It was known locally as Shildon Castle and was home to several families. However, lead mining in the North Pennines was gradually sputtering to a stop. Competition from Europe made the mines less economically viable. In 1883, the Derwent Mining Company, who then owned the Shildon mine, went into liquidation. By the early 20th century, the Shildon Engine House was abandoned as a place of residence and fell into disrepair. That it has been preserved is largely thanks to the North Pennines AONB Partnership and their Living North Pennines project.

Address Clap Shaw, Blanchland, Northumberland, DH8 9SS | Getting there Bus 773 to Lord Crewe Arms or Clap Shaw and then an 11-minute walk; very limited off-road parking nearby | Hours Viewable from the outside only | Tip Hunstanworth – just over the border in County Durham – is a 'Thankful Village' that suffered no fatalities during World War I.

30 Blyth Battery

Watching and waiting…

World War I was the first total war in British history. It affected civilian life in ways that wars had never done before: voluntary service in the armed services was abandoned when conscription began 1916; rationing was introduced in 1917 after Germany began using submarines to cut off Britain's imported food supplies; and the population suddenly found themselves on the front line.

Winged aircraft were too frail and flimsy to bomb Britain in the early years of the war. Death came from the air in the form of Zeppelins, huge dirigible airships capable of carrying a sizeable cargo of bombs. During the war, several towns in north-east England were attacked. Hartlepool was bombed three times, twice in 1916 and once in 1918, when eight people were killed and 22 were injured.

By far the biggest threat, however, was shelling from the North Sea by warships of the German High Seas Fleet. Poor Hartlepool was attacked in this fashion early on the morning of 16 December, 1914, resulting in the deaths of 86 people and 424 injured. To combat this threat, a series of watch towers and gun emplacements were built along the coast from the Tyne to the Tees, of which Blyth Battery is one of the best preserved.

Work began on the battery in August 1916 by the Durham Fortress Engineers. It was fitted with two six-inch Quick Firing guns and two search lights that were manned by the Tynemouth Royal Garrison Artillery. Shells for the guns were stored in the magazine building, which now houses a museum. Curiously, the magazine was built some distance from the guns, rather than adjacent. This was entirely due to the inconvenient nature of the sand dunes on which the battery was built. Also still standing is an observation post built during World War II. So well placed was the battery that when another total war came along, it essentially just needed dusting down and lightly updating.

Address Links Road, Blyth, Northumberland, NE24 3PQ, +44 (0)7881 462284, www.blythbattery.org.uk | Getting there Bus 308 to Links Road; free parking at Mermaid Car Park | Hours Apr–Sep Sat & Sun 11am–4pm | Tip Learn more about the military life in Northumberland at 'Charge! The Story of England's Cavalry', a permanent exhibition in Newcastle's Discovery Museum (www.discoverymuseum.org.uk).

31_Willie Carr Statue

Brawny hands and mighty arms

St George may have slain a dragon but he never lobbed a donkey into a coal-waggon. Willie Carr – the Strongman of Blyth – did. Born on 23 April, 1756, Carr outdid the patron saint in a number of other ways too. According to the 1887 edition of the *Monthly Chronicle of North Country Lore and Legend*, Carr 'was once known to work for 132 consecutive hours, then sleep 12 hours, and resume with unabated vigour for 120 hours more'. And, on one occasion, 'tucked a plump young woman under his arm, and, thus handicapped, leaped a five-barred gate'.

By the time he was 17, Carr stood 'six feet three inches in his stocking feet'. After serving time as a blacksmith's apprentice, he set up in business manufacturing harpoons for the region's whalers. So good were his products that the whalers 'could not satisfy themselves that all was right with them unless they had some of Blyth Willie's implements of fishing as part of their equipment'. By now, Carr had a reputation as a strongman too. His ability to throw 'a weight of sixty pounds a distance of eight yards' brought him to the attention of Lord Delaval of Seaton Delaval Hall. Carr was frequently invited to the estate to display his mighty body and demonstrate his prodigious strength to Delaval's guests.

Despite his size, Carr was described by the *Monthly Chronicle* as 'one of the best tempered men that ever lived, and never otherwise than peaceably disposed'. Therefore, when Carr was menaced by 'vagrant muggers', he did not rush to cause undue physical harm. Instead 'he laid his big hands on their donkey as it was meekly browsing on the thistles by the side of the tramway, and quietly chucked it into an empty coal-waggon, leaving his enraged enemies in great wonder at the feat…'. Carr died on 6 September, 1825 after a long illness. He is commemorated by a handsome statue by Philip Blacker in Blyth's Keel Row.

Address Keel Row Shopping Centre, Regent Street, Blyth, Northumberland, NE24 1AH,
+44 (0)1670 369585, www.keelrow.co.uk | Getting there Bus 1, 308, 309 Cobalt & Coast,
X7 Max and various others to Blyth Bus Station; free parking at Keel Row Car Park |
Hours Mon–Sat 9am–5.30pm, Sun 10am–4pm | Tip Outside The Delaval Arms pub is
the Blue Stone, which was probably once an Anglo-Saxon boundary marker, and which
Willie Carr once picked up to prove his strength (delavalarms.com).

32 Bolam Lake
Planned perection

John Dobson is one of Newcastle's greatest architects. In the first half of the 19th century, he designed iconic buildings such as the Central Station, Eldon Square ('old' Eldon Square that is, not the modern shopping centre), Grainger Market, as well as a good portion of Grey Street. Basically, Dobson, working closely with builder Richard Grainger, was responsible for the stately Neoclassical look of the modern city.

Another of Dobson's creations is Bolam Lake. Though it looks like a natural feature, the lake (and the surrounding woodland) is entirely artificial. In 1816, Dobson was commissioned by John Beresford, a local landowner, to improve his Bolam estate. Curiously, this was the only time in his career that Dobson took on a landscaping project. However, he does appear to have been influenced by 'Capability' Brown. There is no formality to the grounds and nothing feels out of place. The lake replaced a swampy marsh, and is a glittering jewel. The hidden sluices and overflow pipes Dobson designed to maintain the level of the lake work as efficiently today as they did two centuries ago. The woodland, made up of deciduous species such as oak and beech, as well as ornamental conifers, is splendidly organic and unregimented.

So naturalised is the estate that it's a haven for wildlife. Wildfowl, such as swans and ducks predominate, but woodland birds such as fieldfare, redwing, crossbill and waxwing are commonly spotted in the winter months. There is also a significant red squirrel population, an increasingly rare thing in other parts of Northumberland.

Dobson returned to Bolam Lake 30 years after its creation and was horrified by what he saw, lamenting that the trees looked like 'scaffolding poles'. Remedial work was entrusted to Thomas Coxon, a local woodsman. Whatever Coxon did worked, and the region has benefitted ever since.

Address Bolam Lake Country Park, Belsay, Northumberland, NE20 0HE, www.northumberland.gov.uk | Getting there There are three car parks at Bolam Lake: Low House Wood, Boathouse Wood and West Wood. Parking is free for the first hour, with payment required for longer stays | Hours Open during daylight hours (gates locked at dusk) | Tip Jesmond Dene is a woodland park near Newcastle that was gifted to the city by the Victorian industrialist William Armstrong (www.jesmonddene.org.uk).

33___ Shaftoe Crags
Marks on the landscape

At first glance, the Open Access moorland of Shaftoe Crags looks to be a thoroughly wild and untouched place. However, humans have made their mark there in a number of different ways. Look carefully as you wander around the area, and those marks will gradually become apparent.

One of the oldest marks is the remains of an Iron Age (and later Romano-British) settlement above Salter's Nick. The builders of the settlement used the natural features of the landscape – the tall crags of coarse gritstone – as part of the defences. The view from the crags across the flatter landscape beyond is splendid too, ideal for keeping a watch on all who approached. A curved earth and stone rampart can still be made out, as well as evidence for three roundhouses.

A more obvious mark can be found on Piper's Chair at the southern end of Shaftoe Crags. This curiously named rock appears to have had a chunk scooped out to form a very comfortable seat. However, an even stranger mark can be found by carefully clambering up onto the taller and larger rock platform behind Piper's Chair. There you'll find the Devil's Punchbowl, a perfectly circular basin in the surface of the rock. This was originally a natural feature of the rock that was enlarged and neatened off in 1725 on the occasion of the marriage of Sir William Blackett, owner of the nearby Wallington estate, to Lady Barbara Villiers, daughter of the Second Earl of Jersey. On the wedding night, the basin was filled with wine for those celebrating on the hill. Bonfires were then lit on the crags and a 'drink-maddened crowd' partied the evening away.

Another celebratory mark can be found north of Salter's Nick on the moorland above the crags. This is the Jubilee Stone, erected in June 1887 by a Colonel R. Atkinson to honour Queen Victoria on the occasion of her Golden Jubilee. It's unlikely that she knew about the tribute, but Atkinson deserves full marks for the effort.

Address Capheaton, Northumberland, NE61 4EA | **Getting there** Bus X75 to Craig Hall and then a 25-minute walk; small designated area for car parking midway along East Shaftoe Hall farm track and then a 15-minute walk or paid car parking in West Wood Car Park at Bolam Lake (see ch. 32) and then a 35-minute walk | **Tip** Bide-a-Wee is a delightful 'hidden' cottage garden created in a small sandstone quarry by owner Mark Robson (www.bideawee.co.uk).

34__Boulmer

Contraband, cobles and choppers

Boulmer is one of the quieter villages on the Northumberland coast. This may be one reason why it was once a notorious haunt of smugglers and other ne'er-do-wells. During the 1700s, William 'Wull' Faa, King of the Gypsies, boxer and an expert violinist, ran his smuggling operation from the Fishing Boat Inn at the centre of the village. Faa's speciality was the smuggling of gin from Holland that would later be sold in the Scottish Borders. (Wonderfully, a track from Boulmer to Kirk Yetholm, used by Faa and his fellow smugglers, still exists.) Faa's exploits are commemorated in 'The Song of the Smugglers', a local poem about smuggling, which describes how Faa, on one of his less successful jaunts, '…got a great slash i' the hand, When comin' frae Boulmer wi' gin' – presumably, putting a crimp in his fiddling for a short while.

Smuggling ended as a way of life centuries ago, but one traditional industry continues: fishing. Tourists share part of Boulmer's beach with the village's fishing cobles. A coble is a type of fishing boat, developed and used on the coasts of Northumberland and Yorkshire. The two distinctive features of a coble are its flat bottom and high bow. Both features make cobles easier to launch from (and land safely on) the sandy beaches of the region. Remarkably, the design is thought to be influenced by Norse longships. The earliest cobles used a lug sail for propulsion, though modern vessels rely on the less romantic diesel engine.

Boulmer also boasts an RAF station, built during World War II. A variety of aircraft have flown from RAF Boulmer, most notably the Supermarine Spitfires of No. 57 Operational Training Unit. For many years the base was home to 202 Squadron, flying the Sea King helicopters of the RAF's Search and Rescue Force. Now, RAF Boulmer is a vital cog in the UK's Air Surveillance and Control System, monitoring the country's airspace day in and day out.

Address Boulmer, Northumberland, NE66 3BP | Getting there Bus 418 to Fishing Boat; free parking in Boulmer Beach Car Park | Tip The Fishing Boat Inn – no longer frequented by smugglers and ne'er-do-wells – offers food (seafood a speciality) and drink, with a beer 'garden' looking out across the North Sea (www.thefishingboatinn.com).

35 Flodden Field

A Scottish away game

Centuries on, the sites of major battles can be disconcertingly peaceful places. The site of the Battle of Flodden is one such location. On 9 September, 1513, the massed armies of England and Scotland met to duke it out in what would prove to be the largest ever battle between the two nations.

Strangely, relations between King James IV of Scotland and King Henry VIII of England had been relatively cordial. What ignited warfare was Henry's invasion of France in May 1513. Scotland had an agreement with France known as the 'Auld Alliance'. This tied Scotland and France to come to the other's aid should England invade either country. Louis XII, King of France, invoked the treaty and James was compelled to act. And so, some 60,000 Scottish troops crossed the River Tweed, armed in the continental style with pike – described as 'keen and sharp spears 5 yards long'.

Unfortunately for Scotland, Henry had been canny and only used troops from southern England for his invasion of France. Under the command of Thomas Howard, Earl of Surrey, roughly 26,000 English troops from the northern counties marched to meet the Scots. Howard, 70 at the time of the battle, was an experienced soldier and manoeuvred his men north of the Scottish troops, cutting off their retreat back across the Tweed. The two armies met at Branxton Hill, the Scots on higher ground, which should have given them a tactical advantage. It did them no good. The English, armed with bills – a curved blade at the end of a pole – won the battle. Although 1,500 English soldiers were killed, around 10,000 to 17,000 Scots were cut down. To make matters worse for Scotland, James was killed in the battle, along with a good number of Scottish noblemen. The result for Scotland was devastating, and led to political upheaval for decades afterwards. And the site of the battle? It is now farm fields, with only the singing of birds to disturb the silence.

Address Branxton, Cornhill-on-Tweed, Northumberland, TD12 4SS | **Getting there**
Bus 710 to Village Centre and then a short walk; free parking at Flodden Field Memorial
Car Park; from the car park is a short way-marked battlefield trail including a path to a
memorial cross | **Tip** A touching memorial to the battle can be seen in St Paul's Church in
Branxton. Engraved on glass panels are depictions of an English oak and a Scots Pine to
symbolise the centuries-long peace between the two nations (www.stpaulsbranxton.org).

36 Rothley Castle
Not a castle

Thanks to the bad-tempered animosity between England and Scotland during the Middle Ages, Northumberland has more than its fair share of castles and fortified buildings. You therefore couldn't be faulted for thinking that Rothley Castle near Scots Gap is just another medieval stronghold. In fact, it's anything but. It is a folly, built in the 18th century in a deliberately ruinous state.

Rothley Castle was designed by Daniel Garrett in 1755 for Sir Walter Calverley Blackett, then owner of Wallington estate near the village of Cambo. Calverley Blackett was an aristocrat and Tory politician who represented Newcastle in Parliament, and who was mayor of the town five times, earning himself the nickname 'King of Newcastle'.

Walter Calverley was born in 1707. He acquired his double-barrelled status (and Wallington) after marrying Elizabeth Ord, the illegitimate daughter of Sir William Blackett. Blackett had stipulated in his will that, within 12 months of his death, Elizabeth was to marry Calverley, her cousin and nephew of Blackett. It was also a condition of the will that Calverley then had to take the Blackett name, which he was evidently more than happy to do. The couple married in 1729, within the required year of Blackett's passing.

Taking ownership of Wallington estate was a mixed blessing. Sir William had led an extravagantly dissolute life and he died in debt, with Wallington having fallen into disrepair as a result. That Calverley Blackett turned round the estate's fortunes is a testament to his intelligence and skill. So successful was Calverley that he was able to extensively remodel the splendid house at Wallington, improve roads in the area, build the Shambles covered market in Hexham, and to have a number of substantial follies built on his land. Completely useless it may be, but Rothley Castle is a wonderfully eccentric reminder of a truly remarkable man.

Address Rothley, Morpeth, Northumberland, NE61 4JU | **Getting there** Parking at Rothley Cross Roads and then a 30-minute walk along a road, down a farm track and then across Open Access moorland | **Tip** Another of Calverley Blackett's follies is Codger Fort, which overlooks the B6342 just under a mile north of Rothley Castle.

37__Cateran Hole
'Were we going direct to the interior of the Earth?'

Professor Otto Lidenbrock is the eccentric hero of Jules Verne's epic fantasy novel *Journey to the Centre of the Earth*. Lidenbrock, along with his nephew Axel, travel to Iceland and the crater of the Snæfellsjökull volcano. From there, with their guide, Hans Bjelke, they descend down a shaft, eventually reaching a lost world deep beneath the surface of the Earth. After many adventures, including an encounter with a herd of mastodon, the intrepid trio eventually pop up on the Italian island of Stromboli atop a column of water that pushes them and their raft out of a volcanic chimney.

The Cateran Hole, a cave found in otherwise featureless Northumbrian heather moorland, won't lead to similar exciting escapades. It is, however, satisfyingly mysterious. For one thing, although the cave is natural, there are stone steps leading down to the entrance. Who put these here and why?

The accessible length of the Cateran Hole is roughly 115 feet, though local legend has it that the cave once linked Chillingham Castle (see ch. 38) with Hepburn. (Another legend has it stretching to Hen Hole in the Cheviots, some 10 miles away.) It is a mass-movement cave in Fell Sandstone, created not by erosion but when one face of a natural fracture pulled away from the other. What caused movement in the rock where the cave formed is another of its mysteries.

The entrance has been worked at some point and 1765 carved into a flat ledge of rock, creating another puzzle. One theory is that the cave was once a useful hideout for smugglers in the 18th century. Another possibility is suggested by the name of the cave. Cateran is a Scottish term describing a band of fighting men. This could easily be a synonym for the Border Reivers, who would have been grateful for such a well-hidden bolthole when the law was breathing down their necks.

Address Cateran Hill, Quarryhouse Moor, near Chillingham, Northumberland, NE66 4EG | Getting there Limited parking near the Quarryhouse Moor footpath to Cateran Hole; a torch, sturdy boots and hard hat are highly recommended, particularly if you intend to explore the full length of the cave | Tip Nearby Ros Castle is the highest point on the moors surrounding Chillingham and has an excellent view across to the Cheviots in the west. There is no castle there but traces of an Iron Age settlement can be found.

38 Chillingham Castle
Spooky

Chillingham Castle dates back to the 13th century and, like many castles in Northumberland, was involved in the various Anglo-Scottish disagreements during the medieval period. King Henry III came to Chillingham Castle in 1245, and King Edward I stayed there in 1298 on his way north to fight the Battle of Falkirk. More happily, King James VI of Scotland stopped off at the castle on his way south to be crowned King James I of England. Despite this history, though, the castle is arguably better known as the most haunted historic castle in Britain. So infamous is it that ghost tours quickly sell out, particularly those held in the dead of night.

The ghosts take a number of forms. There are figures regularly seen in particular places, inside and outside the castle. And visitors have reported a variety of odd phenomena, such as sensing unseen movement, hearing voices, or experiencing creeping dread.

The ghostly figures have names: the Radiant Boy, the White Pantry Ghost, and the Grey Lady. The latter is the restless spirit of Lady Mary Berkeley, who fruitlessly spends eternity searching for her unfaithful husband, Lord Grey of Werke. Scandalously, the philandering lord had an affair with Lady Mary's younger sister, Henrietta. Poor Lady Mary died at Chillingham Castle aged 31, possibly (and understandably) of a broken heart. Witnesses have reported hearing the rustle of her silk dress as she passes by, followed by a sharp drop in the ambient temperature.

The Radiant Boy is the spirit of a child seen in the Pink Room, whose cries of pain are heard when midnight chimes. The apparition appears in a dazzling flash of light, apparently from the direction of one particular wall. The bones of a child were later found behind this wall and given a Christian burial. The nocturnal visits stopped until the room was let out. Obviously objecting to this, the Radiant Boy returned and has been waking guests ever since.

Address Chillingham, Northumberland, NE66 5NJ, +44 (0)1668 215359, www.chillingham-castle.com | Getting there Free parking at Chillingham Castle | Hours Apr–Oct 11am–5pm; evening ghost tours and ghost hunts also available (see website) | Tip The Chatton Gallery is a showcase for the local landscape paintings of Robert Turnbull (www.thechattongallery.com).

39 Chillingham Cattle
Mooving experience

Northumberland has its own unique breed of cattle, one that is untamed and free from human interference (not even veterinary care). The Chillingham Cattle are truly wild and can only be seen in the company of an experienced guide. The animals are relatively small and lean compared with modern cattle breeds, because they've never been 'improved' by selective breeding over the centuries. They also have a wonderfully crisp and shaggy white coat, and sport long, curved horns on their head.

One – now abandoned – theory was that the cattle were aurochs, the ancestral animal from which domesticated cattle were bred. What is known is that the cattle have lived in splendid isolation on the Chillingham estate for nearly 800 years. Originally, they were game animals, hunted for sport with hounds and lances. Able to run at 30 miles per hour and ill-tempered, the cattle would have presented a formidable challenge to even the most experienced hunter.

There are approximately 130 cattle in the herd. However, natural pressures do have their effect on numbers. The herd dropped to a dangerously low 13 animals after the brutally hard winter of 1947. The Foot and Mouth outbreaks of 1967 and 2001 also presented a challenge. Strict biosecurity measures were established during the latter occurrence to keep the herd free of the disease. There is now a 'backup' herd in a secret location in Scotland just in case.

Because of the small size of the herd, the Chillingham Cattle are essentially clones of each other. This is not due to sinister scientific experimentation but because there is no outbreeding, the usual solution to widening a gene pool. Strangely, despite this lack of genetic diversity, there are very few birth defects. Calves born with physical abnormalities are quickly abandoned by their mothers and die. From a human perspective this may seem cruel but the Chillingham Cattle are nothing if not survivors.

Address Near St Peter's Church, Chillingham, Northumberland, NE66 5NP, +44 (0)1668 215250, chillinghamwildcattle.com | **Getting there** Parking at the Chillingham Wild Cattle Park | **Hours** Regular daily tours from Easter–Oct | **Tip** Belford Museum is an ever-evolving museum run by enthusiastic volunteers that features information and exhibits that tell the history of the village (www.belfordmuseum.co.uk).

40_ St Andrew's Church
A long history

Our ancestors were wise and recycled resources long before it was the environmentally friendly thing to do. Many a page of text would be washed or scraped off so that the paper or parchment could be reused. A page used more than once in this way is known as a palimpsest. Often the faint traces of older text can still be read, providing modern researchers with valuable information that may otherwise have been lost. Old buildings are often essentially a palimpsest too, with original features almost but not quite erased by later modifications.

St Andrew's Church in Corbridge is such a building. A church has stood on the site since the seventh century, founded by St Wilfrid, who also had a hand in the founding of Hexham Abbey. The stone used to build this church probably came from the nearby Roman town of Corstopitum, abandoned in the fifth century when the Roman Empire excused itself from Britain. Traces of the original church can be seen in the tower and baptistry, which would once have been the western entrance to the church. (The stained-glass windows in the baptistry are where the door would once have been.) It's believed that the curved arch over the interior entrance to the baptistry was taken wholesale from Corstopitum.

Most of the rest of St Andrew's dates from the 13th century, when Corbridge was a thriving and prosperous town. This wealth paid for extensive remodelling of the church, creating the layout seen today. Unfortunately, in 1296, a Scottish army invaded the area, laying waste to Corbridge and badly damaging St Andrew's. Subsequent Scottish invasions over the next 20 years resulted in further ruination to the structure of the building. Although some repairs were made to the church over the centuries, it was only in 1867, after a four-year rebuilding project, that St Andrew's was fully restored to its current glory.

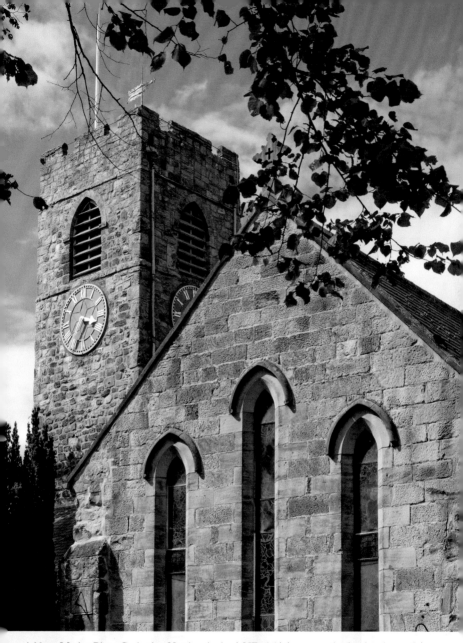

Address Market Place, Corbridge, Northumberland, NE45 5AA, www.corbridgechurch.org.uk |
Getting there Bus 684 Tynedale Links to Market Square; free parking in Corbridge Village
Car Park and then a short walk; train to Corbridge then a 12-minute walk | **Hours** Daily
8.30am–5pm except Christmas Day | **Tip** The neighbouring Vicar's Pele is a fortified house,
built during the period of the Anglo-Scottish wars. It's now a micro pub serving locally made
brews, as well as lagers and ciders (www.thepele.co.uk).

41 Walker's Pottery
Cone, but not forgotten

Industrial buildings are rarely thought of as beautiful. The two brick bottle kilns of Walker's Pottery are the exception. They date back to the 19th century and were used for the firing of bricks, tiles and clay pipes. Their gently curved shape resembles a traditional beehive, though a beehive some 50 feet high. Step through the doorway of one of the kilns and look up. The chimney aperture at the top provides useful light to appreciate the wonderfully precise and regular structure of the interior.

Walker's Pottery closed in the early 20th century. The pottery's bottle kilns are remarkable survivors, a rarity in the north east. Originally there were three bottle kilns but one was demolished sometime in the 1890s. The clay for the pottery was sourced locally, probably from a (now disused) clay pit roughly 800 feet north east of the site. The raw clay would have been transported along a tramway, of which some 165 feet still survives, though now buried out of sight underground. At the pottery, the clay would be mixed with water in a puddling pit. Sand would also be added to temper the clay, to make it easier to work and improve its firing qualities. The shaped clay products were stored in a drying room, kept warm by underfloor heating. This protected the products from the risk of frost damage before they were fully hardened by firing in the kilns.

Not all of Walker's Pottery is accessible. Other buildings – the workshops, a drying shed and machine room – are on private property. Some can be seen, however, from the kilns, in a ruined state but still standing. One of these buildings is a large stable block where the pottery's horses and carts were kept. These would have been used to deliver the finished clay products along the Tyne Valley. Wonderfully, the horses' troughs are still there and were probably made at the pottery. Whether the horses appreciated this will, sadly, never be known.

Address Milkwell Lane, Corbridge, Northumberland, NE45 5QF | **Getting there** Bus 684 Tynedale Links or 885 to Prior Terrace and then a 15-minute walk; very limited on-street parking nearby | **Hours** Viewable from permissible path only | **Tip** Established in 1878, Errington Reay is the only commercial pottery in Britain still making traditional salt glaze pottery (www.erringtonreay.co.uk).

42 _The Giant Spoon
A stirring sight

Close your eyes and imagine a farm field. You'll probably picture acres of golden wheat, gently waving in the wind. Or possibly lambs scampering playfully in spring sunshine. What you're unlikely to visualise is a 15-foot dessert spoon standing upright and embedded into the ground as though it had somehow fallen from a great height. If you did, you either have a *very* odd imagination indeed or you're the artist Bob Budd.

In 2006, Budd created the sculpture for a lottery-funded art trail. Entitled *Eat for England*, the piece is more commonly known locally as *The Giant Spoon*. And rightly so, for that is exactly what it is. Rather than place it on a busy high street, Budd chose to have his sculpture erected next to a footpath on the edge of a farm field in Cramlington. The piece, he hoped, would be a 'carrot' to encourage people to explore this quiet corner of Northumberland, a hope that has been more than fulfilled in the years since.

Eat for England was placed where it was for another reason. The location is a gentle reminder that food doesn't just magically arrive on our plates. Crops have to be sown and, when ripe, need to be harvested, processed and transported to market. This activity is largely hidden from public view, so it is a rare person indeed who can definitively say where their meals come from.

The title is also a deliberate nod to the phrase 'Dig for Victory', devised by the Ministry of Agriculture in World War II. During the war – and for some years afterwards – food was rationed to ensure a fair share for all. Public parks were dug up and essentially transformed into giant allotments. The public was also encouraged to dig up flower gardens and lawns to plant vegetables. It worked, and no one in Britain starved. In fact, many people had a healthier, more nutritious, diet than before the war. Which, in an age of ready meals laden with fat and sugar, is surely food for thought.

Address Cramlington, Northumberland, NE23 7TL | Getting there Bus 57A or X7 Max to Bay Horse and then a 10-minute walk from the B1505, through an underpass below the A189 and along a public footpath; on-street parking off the B1505 near the Bay Horse Inn | Tip East Cramlington Local Nature Reserve is home to a wide range of amphibians, including frogs, newts and toads, as well as birds such as skylark, song thrush, linnet and yellowhammer (www.naturalengland.org.uk).

43 _Northumberlandia_
Mother Earth

What is the largest figurative sculpture in north-east England? Deduct five points if you said the _Angel of the North_ (see ch. 60). Go to the top of the class and award yourself a gold star if _Northumberlandia_ was your answer. _Northumberlandia_ – or the 'Lady of the North' – is a landform sculpture of a reclining woman. Built using 1.5 million tonnes of soil, stone and clay, she is 1,300 feet long and 112 feet high at her highest point (her forehead in case you were wondering). Four miles of footpaths loop sinuously around her body and the surrounding countryside, up on to a viewing platform that lets you see the various parts of her grassy body.

The building material came from the Shotton Surface Mine, which opened in 2007. _Northumberlandia_ and her community park were proposed as legacy projects in 2004, when the owners of the land – Banks Group and Blagdon Estates – applied for planning permission to open the mine. Work was completed in 2012, and the park was opened by Princess Anne on 4 September that year. On unveiling a plaque at the entrance, the princess said 'I hope that many more generations will appreciate her and the fact she is so different from anything anywhere in the universe'. (Which is a hard claim to verify, but probably true…)

Northumberlandia was designed by the American artist Charles Jencks, who lived in Britain for over 50 years until his death in 2019. Jencks was renowned for his large-scale landscape architecture projects, which were often inspired by fractals and the implications of chaos theory. The design of _Northumberlandia_ was influenced by the round shapes of the Cheviots (see ch. 84), which on a clear day are visible from the site. One thing that now cannot be seen is Shotton Surface Mine. For eight years it was possible to see into the vast hole from _Northumberlandia_, but this hole was filled in and landscaped when the mine closed in 2020.

Address Blagdon Lane, Cramlington, Northumberland, NE23 8AU, www.northumberlandia.com | Getting there Bus X21 Sapphire or X22 Sapphire to Fisher Lane roundabout and then a 13-minute walk; free parking at *Northumberlandia* (though a donation of £2 is appreciated) | Hours Daily dusk–dawn (café open 10am–4pm, closed Christmas Day and Boxing Day) | Tip The Northumberland Cheese Company sells local handmade cheese from their farmhouse shop (www.northumberlandcheese.co.uk).

44 Turner's View

Artistic leanings

Joseph Turner is known as 'the painter of light' for his wondrously luminous landscape paintings. Born in London in 1775, he was a child prodigy who enrolled at the Royal Academy Schools at the age of 14 and exhibited his first work there, *A View of the Archbishop's Palace, Lambeth*, one year later. Turner travelled extensively during his life, filling sketchbooks with pencil and watercolour sketches that would later be used as reference for larger watercolours and oil paintings. One location that would prove to be particularly inspirational was Dunstanburgh Castle on Northumberland's coast.

Turner recorded views of Dunstanburgh Castle in his 'North of England' sketchbook of 1797. Although he only visited Dunstanburgh once, it was a subject he returned to many times afterwards, possibly more than any other subject. For Turner, Dunstanburgh Castle was a perfect metaphor for the passing of time and the power of nature. However, he wasn't above embellishing the view, and many of his paintings of the castle have numerous craggy details not found then or now. Turner's 1799 oil painting, *Dunstanborough Castle, Northumberland*, is an atmospheric piece depicting a storm-tossed sea with the castle framed by a dramatic sky. It is also oddly but wonderfully inaccurate geographically.

Strangely, Dunstanburgh Castle was a relative failure, which is why it was ruinous by Turner's time. It was built in the early 14th century by Thomas, Earl of Lancaster. Dunstanburgh was then improved by John of Gaunt in the 1380s, for this was the time of the Anglo-Scottish wars. However, the size of the castle and its distance from the Scottish Border eventually counted against it. Expensive to maintain, by the 15th century the structure was decaying and largely abandoned. But then, arguably, without this change in fortune, Turner would not have found artistic inspiration on his one and only visit…

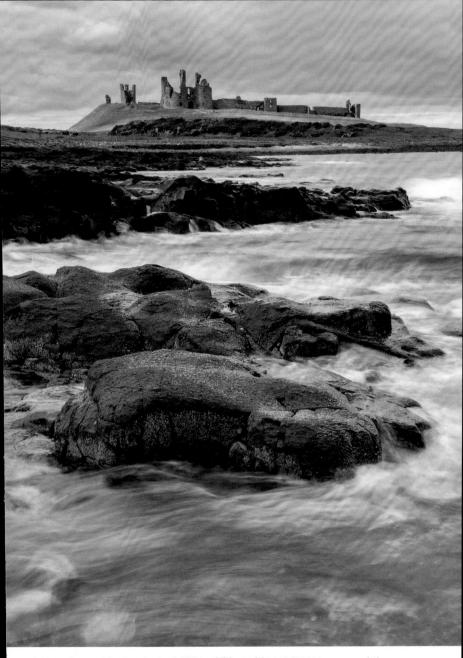

Address Craster, Northumberland, NE66 3TT, +44 (0)1665 576231, www.english-heritage.org.uk | Getting there Bus 418 or X18 Max to Harbour and then a 25-minute walk; paid parking at Craster Car Park and then a 25-minute walk | Hours Castle open Apr–Oct daily 10am–5pm, Nov–Mar Sat & Sun 10am–4pm | Tip See the work of self-taught seaside artist Mick Oxley in his gallery in Craster (www.mickoxley.com).

45 __ Hemscott Hill Pillbox

Hidden in plain sight

You could be forgiven for thinking that a small derelict building on the Druridge Bay road is an abandoned cottage. Look closely though and you'll note the strangely small windows and the thickness of the walls. This is no cottage. It is a pillbox, purpose built during World War II.

Invasion by German forces was a constant fear during the early stages of the war. The long and relatively remote beach at Druridge Bay was seen as a potential landing point for invasion barges. Standard designs for pillboxes were issued in June 1940 by the War Office Directorate of Fortifications and Works. Many of these were installed along the east coast of England, as well as at strategic points inland. The Hemscott Hill pillbox is unique, due to its position slightly inland from the beach.

At only 40 feet high, Hemscott Hill is a slight misnomer. However, whatever is built on its 'summit' stands out in the flat surrounding landscape. If a conventional pillbox had been built on Hemscott Hill it would have been an immediate target for destruction by invaders. The cottage design of the Hemscott Hill pillbox is therefore a cunning disguise, which would have bought British defenders precious time to counterattack. And everything about the pillbox is fake. The brick chimney never worked. The apparently missing roof never existed. (There is a roof, but it's flat, made of corrugated concrete and invisible from the outside.) And the windows were never windows, but narrow gun embrasures.

There were many other defences built along the Northumbrian coast, including conventional pillboxes and concrete tank traps. Many of these are now gone, either removed post-war or having long fallen into dereliction. Due to its unique design, Hemscott Hill pillbox is a listed building. Not only did it survive the war, but it now has a fighting chance of standing for many years to come.

Address Hemscott Hill, Widdrington, Northumberland, NE61 5EQ | Getting there Free parking at the Beach Car Park and then a short walk | Tip Druridge Bay Country Park is a splendid place for a walk and a picnic, and boasts a visitor centre, large freshwater lake and children's play area (www.northumberland.gov.uk).

46 Duddo Five Stones
Ancient architecture

If you need to navigate outdoors then there is nothing more satis-fyingly precise than an Ordnance Survey map. The OS has a well-deserved reputation for accuracy, and their maps are updated regularly to take account of changes in the landscape. This makes the name Duddo Four Stones, a small stone circle shown on OS Explorer map 339, all the more puzzling. Everyone – apart from the OS – refers to the site as Duddo Five Stones for the undeniably sensible reason that there are *five* stones standing there.

Just to confuse things, there would once have been six stones. (Or possibly seven – opinions strangely vary on the matter.) In the approximately 4,000 years since the original construction of the cir-cle, one (or two) of the stones has (or have) vanished without trace; a large gap at the western edge of the circle indicates where the missing stone (or stones) once stood.

The five stones do now look their age. Made of sandstone, each has been deeply scored by weathering over the millennia. However, some of the markings may have been carved intentionally, their mes-sage now lost to history (rather like the cup-and-ring marked rocks found elsewhere in the county). Why the circle was placed where it was is also a mystery, though the splendid view for miles around is one possible and plausible explanation.

So, why does the OS still refer to the circle as Duddo Four Stones? When it was first excavated in the 1890s there were only four stones standing. An 1899 edition of the Ordnance Survey map for the area therefore logically identifies the site as Duddo Four Stones (Stone Circle) (Remains of). Then, in 1903, the fifth stone – which had merely fallen over – was re-erected, for aesthetic reasons rather than scientific. The OS, for reasons of their own, insist on sticking with the old name. It may take them another 120 years or so to finally catch up with the locals, but, who's counting?

Address Duddo, Berwick-upon-Tweed, Northumberland, TD15 2PT | **Getting there** Bus 267 to Tower Cottage and then a 25-minute walk along a permissive path through farm fields; limited parking on the verge next to the first field gate and then a 20-minute walk | **Tip** Heatherslaw Light Railway connects Heatherslaw and the village of Etal. The line's steam and diesel locomotives are operated between March and October, as well as for 'Santa Specials' in the run-up to Christmas (www.heatherslawlightrailway.co.uk).

47 Hartley Pit Memorial
Names carved in stone

Winter had Northumberland in its grip. The morning of 16 January, 1862 was bitterly cold. Men and boys alike must have grumbled as they walked in the half-light to start their shift at Hartley (or Heter) Pit near the village of Earsdon.

The pit was sunk in 1830 so that three extensive coal seams could be worked. The miners reached the seams down a single shaft some 12-feet across. Due to its proximity to the North Sea, the mine was prone to flooding. In 1858, a massive 400-horsepower steam pumping engine was installed that was able to pump water 240 feet vertically up the shaft. So big and powerful was the pump that its cast-iron supporting main beam weighed 40 tons.

At 10am, deep underground, the new shift replaced the old. It was then that the main beam cracked and snapped. Two miners who were travelling up in the cage were killed instantly, with three later dying from their wounds. The debris also completely blocked the shaft, trapping the two shifts in the pit. Miners from nearby pits rushed to help but progress was slow. The discovery of poisonous fumes hampered efforts further and so it took six agonising days to reach the trapped miners.

Everyone was dead. Some 199 men and boys, their lives snuffed out by the very fumes that had slowed down the relief effort. The rescuers who found the bodies reported that the dead looked as though they were merely sleeping. A tin flask was found with the words *Mercy, oh God!* scratched into its surface; another poignantly read 'Friday afternoon. My Dear Sarah, – I leave you'. Virtually every family in the area was affected by the disaster, with one family – the Liddles – losing nine members at a stroke. Most of the victims were buried in the churchyard of St Albans in Earsdon, with 60,000 people attending the funeral procession on 26 January. A memorial inscribed with the victims' names was erected later that year.

Address St Alban's Church, Front Street, Earsdon, Northumberland, NE25 9JX | Getting there Bus 51 to Front Street or Garden Terrace; Metro to West Monkseaton (Yellow line) and then a 22-minute walk; limited on-street parking opposite St Alban's | Tip Nearby Church Way was where Scottish eccentric Angus McSporran (Billy Connolly) proposed to Granny 'Supergran' Smith (Gudrun Ure) in the first series of *Supergran*, produced in 1985 by Tyne Tees.

T. CLEDSON.	ACED 16	MACFARLANE. ACED 24
T. CLEDSON.	ACED 40	J. MCKEE. ACED 15
W. LIDDLE.	ACED 17	A. MCKEE. ACED 55
W. LIDDLE.	ACED 19	W. MCCRACHEN. ACED 24
J. LIDDLE.	ACED 16	R. NORTH. ACED 24
J. LIDDLE.	ACED 18	C. NORTH. ACED 26
T. LIDDLE.	ACED 16	J. NORTH. ACED 10
C. LIDDLE.	ACED 11	A. NORTH. ACED 14
J. LIDDLE.	ACED 11	J. NICHOLSON. ACED 32
T. LIDDLE.	ACED 19	J. NICHOLSON. ACED 21
T. LIDDLE.	ACED 19	J. ORMSTON. ACED 32
T. LAWS.	ACED 33	P. NESBIT. ACED 20
C. LAWS.	ACED 23	J. NICHOLSON. ACED 14
W. LOUCE.	ACED 30	W. OLIVER. ACED 56
J. LONC.	ACED 15	J. OLIVER. ACED 27
R. LONC.	ACED 17	J. OLIVER. ACED 21
M. MURRAY.	ACED 28	W. OLIVER. ACED 17
R. MURLEY	ACED 23	P. OLIVER. ACED 15
		T. PEARSON. ACED 28

48__Ford and Etal
Estate planning

Post-war new towns such as Milton Keynes – or Killingworth, for that matter – suffer a great deal of often unfair derision. For some reason, people seem to find the idea of a community created entirely from scratch as highly amusing. Ford, an estate village in north Northumberland, is a charming exception.

In 1859, the Ford estate was inherited by Lady Louisa Waterford on the death of her husband, Henry Beresford, Third Marquess of Waterford. The original village of Ford was merely a handful of decrepit cottages. On taking charge, the far-sighted Lady Waterford had the village completely rebuilt in order to provide better, more substantial and aesthetically pleasing new houses for her estate workers, as well as a new school for their children.

Lady Waterford was a very talented watercolour artist who was an admirer of the Pre-Raphaelite Brotherhood. She spent 21 years decorating the interior of the new school with murals depicting characters and scenes from the Bible. Touchingly, she used the people of Ford as her models. The school closed in 1957 and is now open to the public as the Lady Waterfall Hall.

The village of Etal is just a few minutes' drive from Ford. Ford and Etal were two separate estates until 1908 when James Joicey, First Baron Joicey, bought Etal, having bought the Ford estate the previous year. More than a century on, the two estates are still owned by the Joicey family. For that reason, Ford is now rarely mentioned without also including Etal, and vice versa. Unlike Ford, Etal was not planned, and grew up under the protection of Etal Castle, built shortly after the Norman Conquest. Though small, Etal does have one thing found nowhere else in Northumberland: a thatched pub. The Black Bull is thought to be almost 700 years old, the building first used to house prisoners who had been sentenced to death at Etal Castle.

Address Ford, Berwick-upon-Tweed, Northumberland, TD15 2QG or Etal, Cornhill-on-Tweed, TD12 4TL, www.ford-and-etal.co.uk | **Getting there** Bus 267 to Bank Top (Ford) or to Village entrance (Etal); on-street parking in both villages | **Hours** The Lady Waterford Hall is open daily 11am–4pm | **Tip** Etal Castle is a ruined medieval castle where you can see an award-winning exhibition about the Battle of Flodden in the old Presbyterian chapel (www.english-heritage.org.uk).

49 Range Towers
Boooom!

Northumberland has many beautiful sandy beaches that are often strangely empty even at the height of summer. This is usually because the beaches are some distance from the nearest road, or from the sort of facilities expected by modern holidaymakers. Cheswick and Goswick Sands near Berwick are typical. However, it's not so very long ago that these two beaches were *deliberately* kept clear of people. The evidence for this is two derelict brick and concrete towers, one each nestled in the dunes of the two beaches.

RAF Milfield, north of the Cheviots, opened in early 1942 at the height of World War II. It was manned from August 1942 by 59 Operational Training Unit, who worked in conjunction with nearby RAF Brunton to train pilots for ground attack and dive-bombing missions. The pilots at Milfield flew Miles Master and Magister training aircraft, as well as Hawker Hurricanes, a front-line fighter aircraft during the Battle of Britain but, by 1942, outclassed by new German fighter aircraft and so on the verge of obsolescence.

By spring, 1944 planning was well underway for D-Day, the day on which the Allied invasion of Europe would be launched. Hawker Typhoon and Tempest aircraft were now stationed at Milfield so that pilots could practise with the types beforehand. The Typhoon was particularly suited to ground attack, armed as it was with cannon, and able to carry bombs and rockets under its wings.

Where could the pilots train for war? This is where the towers enter into the story. Goswick Sands was essentially used as an artillery range by the pilots of RAF Milfield. Old armoured vehicles were even placed on the beach as targets. The towers were used to observe firing runs and check how accurate (or not) the pilots were. So much ordnance was dropped or fired that RAF disposal regularly removed live ammunition from the beach for decades after the war, including seven 500-pound bombs found in 2009.

Address Berwick-upon-Tweed, Northumberland, TD15 2RW | Getting there Free parking at Cheswick Sands Car Park and then a 25-minute walk along the beach to the Cheswick quadrant tower or a 45-minute walk to Goswick quadrant tower | Hours Viewable from the outside only | Tip The Barn at Beal offers a wide range of food and drink options, as well as a splendid view across Holy Island Sands (barnatbeal.com).

50 Black Carts

'None shall pass!'

Emperor Hadrian had an idea. He would build a wall on the island of Britannia, at the north-western edge of his empire. The wall would be both a physical and psychological barrier, displaying in solid stone the might and ambition of Rome. And so, in A.D. 122, Hadrian sailed up the River Tyne to see the country where his wall would be built. It took six years or so but, when complete, it stretched 73 miles across the country, from the Tyne to the Solway Firth. Not that Hadrian stuck around all that time. His was a flying visit only, for emperors don't need to get their hands dirty *actually* building things.

Nothing lasts forever. Nearly 300 years later, the Roman Empire, striven by both internal and external pressures, began to crack and fall apart. In A.D. 407, the Romans abandoned Britannia, leaving the natives to fend for themselves. Hadrian's impressive wall was thus surplus to requirements. The stone it was made from was too valuable a resource to ignore, however. And so, gaps appeared in the wall, the purloined stone cannily used to build churches, farm houses and, in the 18th century, the Military Road between New-castle and Carlisle.

Huge chunks of Hadrian's Wall are now long gone. A satisfyingly lengthy stretch can be found at Black Carts, however, as can a fine example of a turret (29A) too. The wall at Black Carts is roughly eight feet deep, making it 'narrow wall'. When construction started in the east, Hadrian's Wall was built 10 feet deep, a specification known as 'broad wall'. At some point the Romans changed their minds about how the wall should be built. Why they did this is uncertain, though it was probably to save time. Oddly, the turrets and milecastles along Hadrian's Wall were built beforehand, usually with 'broad wall' extensions. Turret 29A has these extensions, which noticeably jut out from the surrounding wall on both sides.

Address B6318, Low Teppermoor, Northumberland, NE46 4DB | Getting there
Black Carts is on the route of the Hadrian's Wall Path; very limited free parking on the
B 6318 nearby and then a 10-minute walk | Tip Hjem is a Michelin-starred restaurant that
serves Scandinavian food made with local produce and created by Swedish chef Daniel
Berlin Krog (www.restauranthjem.co.uk).

51 Brunton Turret

'In my time, I have been threatened by experts'

Brunton Turret (26B) isn't the best-preserved turret on Hadrian's Wall. Nor is it (arguably) in a particularly dramatic location, unlike other turrets further west. It does, however, have the distinction of having the highest walls still standing of any turret. One of the walls is well above head height, unless you're particularly tall. Brunton Turret is also flanked by a decent stretch of Hadrian's Wall, which helps you see how turrets were integrated into the wall structure. Pleasingly, it's just a few minutes' walk from a handy lay-by on a well-connected road too. If you want to visit every extant turret along the wall, then it's any easy one to tick off.

The turrets along Hadrian's Wall were watchtowers, manned by two or three Roman legionnaires at a time. There were two turrets spaced equally between every milecastle on Hadrian's Wall. As there were 80 milecastles, there were at least 160 turrets in total. However, some pre-existing towers were incorporated into Hadrian's Wall too (Pike Hill in Cumbria being a good example). And turrets were occasionally added long after Hadrian's Wall was completed, such as the extra tower built between Turrets 39A and 39B. Essentially, it's now impossible to say just how many turrets there once were.

This is not the only gap in our knowledge. There would have been two, three or even four floors internally. However, what the roof was like is a complete mystery. Turrets may well have been crenelated like a medieval castle but this has never been confirmed. (A modern reconstruction of a turret at Vindolanda was built with crenelations.) Intriguingly the Rudge Cup, a Roman bronze cup on display in Alnwick Castle (see ch. 4), features a stylised representation of a crenelated turret. But, as is often the case with these things, there is some disagreement as to whether this truly is proof or just Roman artistic licence.

Address Chollerford, Northumberland, NE46 4EJ, www.english-heritage.org.uk | Getting there Brunton Turret is on the route of the Hadrian's Wall Path; bus 680 Tynedale Links, 882 or AD 122 (during the summer months) to Crossroads and then a short walk; free parking on the A 6079 and then a short walk | Tip Chesters is a Hadrianic-era Roman fort completed in A.D. 123, a particular highlight of which is one of the best-preserved Roman bath houses in Britain (www.english-heritage.org.uk).

52 Cuddy's Crags
A wall, running from east to Westeros

Hadrian's Wall was built to consolidate the north-western edge of the Roman empire, creating a permanent barrier between civilisation and the wilder world beyond. Its effect on the natives must have been dramatic, probably evoking fear and awe in equal measure. When built it would have stood at least 16 feet high. Both physically and psychologically it would have been a formidable barrier. The north face may even have been painted white, creating a very visible structure even from some distance.

The stretch of Hadrian's Wall along Cuddy's Crag is a perfect example of why the Romans built the wall where they did. For several miles on either side of the crag, the landscape rises and falls like a rollercoaster. This is due to the Whin Sill formation, an intrusion of dolerite through the underlying beds of sandstone and limestone. Cannily, the Romans used the crags of the Whin Sill as a natural barrier to complement their wall. Dolerite is an igneous rock and extremely resistant to weathering. The Whin Sill is still quarried today in Northumberland, with chips of whinstone used to surface roads. This means that wherever you drive in the country you may well be driving over bits of Northumberland.

In 1981, a young American writer by the name of George R. R. Martin visited Hadrian's Wall. Martin later used this experience as inspiration for The Wall in his fantasy novel series, *A Song of Ice and Fire*, or *A Game of Thrones* as it's more popularly known. At 300 miles in length, 700 feet tall and 300 feet thick, The Wall is a more impressive barrier than Hadrian's more modest effort. It's also made of ice and is over 8,000 years old. The Wall protects the Seven Kingdoms, preventing invasion by heathens from the north. Sound familiar? The Wall (in the TV series) was eventually breached by the Army of the Dead and a handy fire-breathing dragon. Which was a very different fate from that of Hadrian's Wall…

Address Near Housesteads, Haydon Bridge, Northumberland, NE47 6NN | **Getting there** Cuddy's Crag is on the route of the Hadrian's Wall Path; bus AD 122 in the summer months to Housesteads and then a 30-minute walk; paid parking at Housesteads | **Tip** Housesteads is a large Roman fort, built during the construction of Hadrian's Wall to house roughly 800 men. Not only is it one of the most complete Roman forts in Britain, thanks to its position at the top of a hill, it's in a wonderfully dramatic location too (www.english-heritage.org.uk).

53   Milecastle 35

Guarding the frontier

The milecastles on Hadrian's Wall were fortified barracks, built to house the soldiers who carefully watched the unconquered lands to the north. There were once 80 milecastles along the wall, but time and later development have wiped most of them off the map. The best preserved milecastles are found in Northumberland along the Whin Sill stretch of the wall. Milecastle 35 is a particularly fine example. It sits near the summit of the lofty Sewingshields Crag and so has an excellent view for many miles across the surrounding landscape.

Milecastles were built solidly from dressed stone to a height of 17–20 feet, with walls nine feet thick. There were usually two barrack blocks on either side of a central courtyard for the 8–12 soldiers stationed there. Life would have been tough for the men. Milecastles had a small number of amenities but comforts would have been few. The outlines of a hearth as well as a bread oven can be seen at Milecastle 35, but there would have been no loos or baths. It's likely that milecastles supplied the soldiers that manned the smaller (and even less comfortable) turrets on Hadrian's Wall, possibly using a rota system.

Unlike turrets, milecastles were equipped with gateways, one of which opened on the north face of the wall. The gateways allowed traffic to pass through the wall in either direction. It's possible that natives would be charged a toll as they made their way north or south, making a milecastle essentially a lucrative customs post too.

Milecastle 35 may have been the inspiration for the story that King Arthur and his army lie sleeping under Sewingshields Crag, waiting for the day that their country needs them once again. Arthur's sword, Excalibur, is also said to lie at the bottom of nearby Broomlee Lough. However, Milecastle 35 could never be mistaken for Camelot, no matter how hard you squint at it.

Address Near Housesteads, Haydon Bridge, Northumberland, NE47 6NN | Getting there Sewingshields Crag is on the route of the Hadrian's Wall Path; bus AD 122 in the summer months to Housesteads and then a 45-minute walk; paid parking at Housesteads | Tip Other notable milecastles are Milecastle 37 near Housesteads, Milecastle 39 close to Sycamore Gap, and Poltross Burn (Milecastle 48) in the village of Gilsland just over the border in Cumbria.

54 Roman Soldiers

Tabernus super terram

The roughly 10,000 Roman soldiers who manned Hadrian's Wall weren't necessarily Roman. They probably weren't even Italian either. (Or, more accurately, from the boot-shaped country we now know as Italy.) The soldiers largely came from conquered lands in northern Europe, such as Gallia Belgica (Belgium), Germania Superior (Eastern France), as well as from more southerly regions, such as Hispania (Spain) and Mesopotamia (Iraq).

They weren't necessarily legionnaires either, though legionnaires were used to build Hadrian's Wall. Initially, only a Roman citizen could be a legionnaire, so the troops on Hadrian's Wall were largely *auxilia* (auxiliaries). Happily, after 25 years' service, a retiring *auxilia* automatically gained Roman citizenship, with all the rights and privileges that this status brought. This changed in A.D. 212 when Emperor Caracalla granted Roman citizenship to all free men and women in the empire. Ironically, this may have led to a difficulty in army recruitment later in the century. After all, why risk life and limb if there was no juicy reward at the end of your service?

Soldiers were organised into regiments of 500 or 1,000 men. Their principal weapon was the *gladius*, a short but very sharp sword. The *gladius* was typically used in close-quarter fighting, when it could be used to both slash and stab. Another weapon was the *pilum*, a long javelin with a wooden shaft and metal tip. When thrown accurately, a *pilum* would pierce armour very effectively. Infantry benefitted from the protection of a curved rectangular shield or *scutum*, roughly three feet in height. Soldiers could bring these close together in *testudo* (or tortoise) formation, essentially creating a human tank. Cavalry sported a round shield or *clipeus*, which was smaller, lighter and better suited to combat while riding a horse. The story of life as a Roman soldier is wonderfully told at the Roman Army Museum at Greenhead.

Address Roman Army Museum, Carvoran, Greenhead, Northumberland, CA8 7JB, +44 (0)1697 747485, www.vindolanda.com | Getting there The Roman Army Museum is on the route of the Hadrian's Wall Path; bus AD 122 in the summer months to Roman Army Museum; free parking at Roman Army Museum | Hours Daily Feb–Oct 10am–5pm | Tip Vindolanda is a Roman fort and settlement south of Hadrian's Wall. One of the most impressive sites in Hadrian's Wall Country, it's so large that it may take another century to excavate fully (www.vindolanda.com).

55 Wallsend
Wall's end

The modern town of Wallsend is aptly named, for it is situated at the eastern end of Hadrian's Wall. A very short stretch of the wall can still be seen outside the grounds of *Segedunum*, near the starting point of the Hadrian's Wall Path. Originally, the wall would have continued on from here down to the River Tyne, but the missing section was erased when the Swan Hunter Shipyard was built (which – when the remaining shipyard buildings were demolished in the summer of 2022 – is now also lost to history).

The River Tyne was a strategically important stretch of water to the Romans. It would have been used to transport building materials for Hadrian's Wall westwards, at least as far as Prudhoe and possibly even to Hexham, where the river splits into the Rivers North and South Tyne. So important was the Tyne that a fort – *Arbeia* – was built to guard the river's mouth at the northern end of South Shields. *Arbeia* was a supply fort, with goods such as grain arriving on ships of the *Classis Britannica* (Roman British fleet).

The Romans obviously didn't have modern technology to help them plan the route of their wall. By today's standards, their measuring instruments were crude. The main surveying tool was the *groma*, a simple instrument that could be used to calculate distance or whether a line across a landscape was straight. Nevertheless, the Romans were excellent surveyors. The terrain between Wallsend and the Solway Firth would have been thoroughly appraised before the wall was built. The route eventually picked took advantage of natural features such as the Whin Sill formation, or the rivers of northern England. Generally, though, the Romans took the straightest route across country even when this was strategically questionable. They were also sticklers for precision. Milecastles were *always* one Roman mile apart, regardless of how inconvenient this may have been for the builders.

Address Near Segedunum, Wallsend, NE28 6HR | Getting there Bus 12 or 41 Little
Coasters, 40, 42, 42A, 553 or Q3 Quaycity VOLTRA to Wallsend Metro, or 12 to Buddle
Street – Segedunum; Metro Wallsend (Yellow line); free parking at Wallsend Metro | Tip
Segedunum is the name for a Roman fort that was once buried under Victorian workers'
houses. An excellent museum next to the now-excavated fort helps to put Segedunum into
its historical context (www.segedunumromanfort.org.uk).

56 The Forum Cinema
Sound and vision

Monday, 23 August, 1937 had its ups and downs. French neoclassical composer Albert Roussel unfortunately failed to see the day out. A more cheerful episode, however, was the opening of the Forum Cinema in Hexham, an Art Deco replacement for the Gem Picture Palace, which had occupied the site since 1910. A poster promoting the inaugural event proudly proclaimed that the cinema was 'Hexham's New Wonder Theatre', with luxuries such as '4-Colour Stage Lighting' and a 'Western Electric Mirrorphonic Sound System: the standard sound system of the world'.

Patrons paying their two shillings for a seat in the Grand Circle (or six pence to slum it in the Pit) were shown *Keep Your Seats, Please,* starring the irrepressible George Formby. Over the course of 82 fun-filled minutes, Formby sang a number of catchy ditties, one of which was the saucy 'When I'm Cleaning Windows'. The song was promptly banned by a disapproving Lord Reith and the BBC until it was pointed out that Formby had performed it before an appreciative King George VI and Queen Elizabeth at a Royal Variety Performance. It didn't hurt that Queen Mary was a fan too.

Like many cinemas, the Forum suffered when TV came along. Falling attendance resulted in closure between 1974 and 1982, with the auditorium put to use as a bingo hall (a common fate for failed cinemas at the time). It was closed again in the early 1990s after pub chain JD Wetherspoon bought the building. Fortunes improved in 2007 when Hexham Community Partnership acquired the lease. The Forum is now run as a community enterprise, with profits used to improve Hexham and the surrounding area. The cinema has been extensively refurbished in the intervening years too. Improvements include new seating and the installation of a thoroughly modern digital projection and sound system. As a certain cheeky mid-century film star once said, it's turned out nice again.

Address Market Place, Hexham, Northumberland, NE46 1XF, +44 (0)1434 601144, www.forumhexham.com | **Getting there** Bus 680, 683 or 685 Tynedale Links and various others to Monument; train to Hexham and then a short walk; parking on Beaumont Street (requires parking disc available from shops in Hexham) | **Hours** Mon, Wed–Fri & Sun 1.30–9.30pm, Tue 11am–9.30pm, Sat 12.30–9.30pm, check website for times of special events | **Tip** The Victorian Tap is a friendly and informal 19th-century pub that has recently been sensitively refurbished.

57 Painted Panels
May I have the pleasure…?

Hexham Abbey contains many artistic treasures. Perhaps the most striking are the 80 or so medieval painted panels. These are rare survivors of the puritanical Commonwealth period, which began in 1649 at the end of the Second English Civil War. From then, until the restoration of the monarchy in 1660, English churches were systematically purged of 'idolatrous' imagery, with thousands of religious paintings destroyed and statues smashed across the country. The minimalist aesthetic of today's Anglican churches largely dates from this strange and febrile time.

The Abbey's panels depict a variety of religious subjects, including portraits of local saints, as well as those of Christ, the Virgin Mary, and the 12 Apostles. The most ghoulish – to modern sensibilities at least – are four panels found near the Leschman Chapel. These portray a 'Dance of Death' sequence in which a skeletal Death, wielding a sickle, visits in turn a cardinal, a king, an emperor, and finally, a pope. None of the four look particularly thrilled at the prospect of meeting the Grim Reaper. Who would?

The 'Dance of Death' was a common subject in the art of medieval Europe, in literature and poetry, drama and music, as well as pictorially. The aim was to show that death was the great leveller; everyone, no matter how grand a life they led, would one day meet their maker. And, given how short and painful our ancestors' lives could be, it's hardly surprising that the figure of Death loomed large in the medieval imagination.

One message that the 'Dance of Death' did *not* convey was that an individual should make the most of life. Far from it. The 'Dance of Death' was a warning to lead a good and blameless life, and to follow the teachings of the church. Anyone lax enough to ignore the memo was destined to pirouette their way to damnation, there to dance away eternity in an infernal disco without end.

Address Beaumont Street, Hexham, Northumberland, NE46 3NB, +44 (0)1434 602031, www.hexhamabbey.org.uk | **Getting there** Bus 680, 683 or 685 Tynedale Links and various others to Monument; train to Hexham and then a 10-minute walk; parking on Beaumont Street (requires parking disc available from shops in Hexham) | **Hours** Mon–Sat 10am–4pm, Sun 11am–3pm | **Tip** The Frith Stool in Hexham Abbey possibly dates back to the 7th century and the founding of the church by St Wilfrid. Originally a cathedra, or bishop's seat, it was later used by those seeking sanctuary from persecution during the medieval period.

58__The Sele
Central park

The Sele in Hexham is the largest of three adjacent parks in Hexham. However, although low stone walls, gates and a road separate it from the Abbey Grounds and Hexham House Grounds, most people in Hexham just think of all three as the Sele (or Seal, as it's named on old maps). The land was originally granted to the priory of Augustinian canons at Hexham Abbey, which was refounded in 1113, and it remained in their possession until the dissolution of the monasteries in 1537.

In 1753, Sir Walter Calverley Blackett, owner of the Hexham estate, opened the Sele out to the public. According to A. B. Wright's book, *An Essay Towards a History of Hexham*, published in 1823, 'Walks were laid out and trees planted' by Blackett and 'whose public spirit and munificence are remembered with gratitude'. By the early 18th century, the Sele was 'the mall of the fashionables, the privileged playground of the lower classes, and the place of exercise and amusement for all'. In 1908, Lord Allendale, who then owned the land, gifted the park to Hexham Urban District Council, and it has been publicly owned ever since.

The bandstand in the Sele is a wonderful and frequently used Edwardian structure, presented to the town by Henry Bell in 1912. Bell was a local wool merchant, whose father Henry and uncle George, owned a tannery that made Hexham Tans, leather gloves that were exported all around the world. Henry Bell Jnr. was equally successful, and had a distinctive wool warehouse built on Gilesgate. This was recently converted into a complex of apartments, cunningly named The Wool House. By the early 21st century, Bell's bandstand was in a parlous state, with pieces missing from the cast iron decorative features, and with its roof in disrepair. Thanks to a £125,000 refurbishment project in 2016, the bandstand is set for another 100 years of use.

Address Beaumont Street, Hexham, Northumberland, NE46 3LT | Getting there Bus 680, 683 or 685 Tynedale Links and various others to Monument; train to Hexham and then an 11-minute walk; parking on Beaumont Street (requires parking disc available from shops in Hexham) | Hours Always accessible | Tip The Queen's Hall Arts Centre is a library, art gallery and theatre all rolled into one (www.queenshall.co.uk).

59_ The Vault
Hopping venue

Other than in a church, there aren't many places in Northumberland where you can hear music in a medieval setting. The Vault on Hallgate in Hexham is one such place. As the name suggests, The Vault is below street level, reached through an innocuous door at the end of an otherwise unassuming Victorian building. Curiously, though, The Vault would once have been at street level. It's not that the space dramatically sank over the years, it's because the street level rose; possibly when drains and sewers were laid out prior to the construction of the building above in the 19th century.

The Vault was once the ground floor of a medieval brewery, which would have been low and long. The vaulted stone ceiling, which gives the venue its name, was probably added in the 17th century. The floor would have been used to malt grain, a process of germinating grain so that it produces the sugar that is later fermented into alcohol. It's a technique that first developed in the third century A.D. and really only died out 50 years or so ago. Malting grain is a particularly finicky process, requiring careful regulation of temperature and humidity. This was achieved in The Vault through ventilation holes leading up through the roof. These can still be seen – though now converted to windows – just above street level.

Turning what was a disused cellar into an entertainment space was the brainchild of Ben Haslam, established landscape artist and owner of Haslam's of Hexham. Careful restoration and some engineering know-how were needed to create the venue, including the removal of a dividing wall and the installation of a new supporting girder, as well as a lot of cleaning and painting. The Vault was officially opened for business in 2017. Since then (except during lockdown) The Vault has been home to up-and-coming musicians and comedians, as well as more established acts. Ben is also known to take to the stage with his guitar too.

Address 22–24 Hallgate, Hexham, Northumberland, NE46 1XD, +44 (0)1434 603884, www.thevaulthexham.com | Getting there Bus 613, 885 or 889 to Wentworth Car Park; train to Hexham and then a short walk; parking at Wentworth Car Park (requires parking disc available from shops in Hexham) | Hours Only open during concerts and events | Tip The Small World Café is a great place to catch up with friends for a coffee and cake, or have a meal with someone you care about (thesmallworldcafe.com).

60__ The *Shire Angel*
Any old iron?

Gateshead's *Angel of the North* is reckoned to be the UK's most viewed sculpture, visible as it is from a busy stretch of the A1 motorway. It also helps that the *Angel* is 66 feet tall (the height of four double-decker buses), and has a wingspan of 177 feet. Perhaps more impressively, he is made from 200 tonnes of corten steel and can withstand wind speeds up to 100mph thanks to 600 tonnes' worth of concrete foundation. (And the *Angel* definitely *is* a he, based as he is on the body of his creator, Antony Gormley.)

The *Angel of the North* had a rough ride when first commissioned. The proposed design was described as ugly and a waste of the £800,000 it was projected to cost. Local newspapers were sceptical, with the *Evening Chronicle* running a series of dismissive articles. And the *Gateshead Post* ran a cover story comparing the proposed design with *Icarus*, a statue commissioned by Hitler in 1935 and designed by Nazi architect Albert Speer. Even when installed, art experts were sniffy about it. The (now late) critic Brian Sewell waspishly declared at the time that, 'I've seen almost everything else that Antony Gormley has done', and that the *Angel* was 'probably the emptiest, the most inflated, the most vulgar of his works'.

The public quickly came to love the *Angel*, however. He is now a cherished icon of northern England and even rivals the Tyne Bridge as a defining symbol of the region. This is made readily apparent by the number of souvenirs on sale that depict the *Angel* in one form or another. However, no souvenir can compare to the *Shire Angel*, who stands tall over a field near the village of Whitley Chapel. This wonderfully rustic (and rusty) tribute to the original was created by Christopher Hall of Barker House, who used scrap metal to fashion the piece. Although the *Shire Angel* may not have the sheer scale of the original or the audience, he is a delightfully eccentric and witty (country) cousin.

Address Near Barker House, Whitley Chapel, Northumberland, NE46 2JY | Getting there Limited on-street parking in Whitley Chapel and then a 20-minute walk | Hours Viewable from a public footpath | Tip A 1/20 scale model of the *Angel of the North* – created by Gormley as a test piece before the full-sized sculpture – is on display in Gateshead's Shipley Art Gallery (shipleyartgallery.org.uk).

61 St Cuthbert's Cave
Temporary resting place

By A.D. 875, the monks of Lindisfarne had had enough. After almost a century of attacks and raids by bloodthirsty Danes it was time to move to a safer location. So they packed up their precious belongings and left the island. One of their treasures was the body of St Cuthbert, whose resting place had been a draw to pilgrims since his death in A.D. 687.

For eight years the monks moved around northern England, not settling in any one location. Then, in A.D. 883, the monks were given a church in Chester-le-Street in which to lay St Cuthbert. Ironically, their generous patron was a Danish king, who had converted to Christianity and who was devoted to the saint.

The route the monks took during their wanderings is a complete mystery. One clue is two caves in Northumberland, both named St Cuthbert's Cave, where the monks are said to have briefly rested with the saint. The smaller of the two is in an outcrop of sandstone on Doddington Moor. At some point the cave was enlarged. Who did this and why are questions that now cannot be answered. The second, near Holburn, is far more impressive. The cave is created by a huge overhang of sandstone supported on a small rock pillar. It's an atmospheric place, and it's easy to imagine exhausted monks gratefully using the cave as shelter for a night or two.

St Cuthbert remained in Chester-le-Street until the late 10th century. A Danish invasion was again looming, and so the saint's body was moved briefly to Ripon. After a few months, St Cuthbert was carried north once more. According to legend, the cart carrying the coffin abruptly stopped fast in mud. St Cuthbert then appeared to the monks in a vision in which he indicated that he wished to be buried at 'Dunholme', where a dun cow rested. The cow was found high above the River Wear, where Durham Cathedral was eventually built, and where St Cuthbert lies to this day.

Address Holburn, Northumberland, NE70 7PH, www.stcuthbertsway.info | **Getting there** St Cuthbert's Cave is on the route of the St Cuthbert's Way; parking at a National Trust Car Park near Holburn and then a 20-minute walk | **Tip** The St Cuthbert's Way is a 62-mile long-distance walking route between Melrose in the Scottish Borders and Holy Island, linking up sites important in the life of the saint (www.stcuthbertsway.info).

62 Boat Sheds

'Making good use of the things that we find'

Holy Island's harbour is delightfully unkempt, and all the more interesting for it. It's a working harbour, with local fishermen heading out daily to catch crab and lobster. Wander along the shoreline of the harbour and you'll see lobster pots, fishing nets, anchors and floats nestling in the grass. You'll also see a series of wooden boats that have been niftily converted into very spacious storage sheds. The boat sheds are all over 100 years old and many look their age, though they are all maintained to one degree or another.

The boats used to make the sheds were keelboats built from the 1830s onwards to catch herring. The oily fish was once big business for the fishermen of Holy Island. In the late 19th century, 27 five-man keelboats regularly sailed from the harbour. The importance of herring to the island is reflected in the impressive size of a – now converted – smokehouse on Sandham Lane, just a few minutes' walk from the harbour.

The sheds were made by beaching a boat that was no longer seaworthy, flipping it upside down and chopping it in half. The open end was boarded up with planks, and a door added. A layer of tar was then applied to the outside to keep the contents dry. The practice was once common all along the Northumberland coast, but now only the boat sheds on Holy Island survive.

The most pristine boat sheds on the island are the three found next to Lindisfarne Castle, which are replacements for an older trio of boats. The original boats were placed there between 1906 and 1911 during Edwin Lutyens' restoration of the castle (see ch. 63). Two of these boats were replaced by the National Trust in 1980. And then in 2005 two were unfortunately destroyed by arsonists. The National Trust replaced these using an old boat from Leith that was due to be broken up. A few minutes' fun can be had working out which are the replacements and which is the original.

Address Holy Island, Northumberland, TD15 2SW | **Getting there** Holy Island is only accessible at low tide; check the tide times at holyislandcrossingtimes.northumberland.gov.uk before attempting the journey; paid parking at Holy Island Large Car Park | **Tip** Holy Island is small (and flat) enough that the pleasant walk around its circumference – following the public footpath – will only take an hour or two.

63 Lindisfarne Castle

From fortress to a home from home

Scotland has a lot to answer for. Fear of invasion during the many Anglo-Scottish wars resulted in the building of numerous castles and bastles in Northumberland. Lindisfarne Castle is arguably the most aesthetically pleasing example. It proudly sits on an outcrop of dolerite known as Beblowe Crag, part of the long Whin Sill formation that stretches across the county. Take the staircase to the battlements and you can see why the castle was built where it was: Holy Island is otherwise flat and so visibility is good in every direction.

Curiously, the castle was built relatively late as these things go. Construction started in 1570, using stone taken from the abandoned Lindisfarne Priory (see ch. 64). Its role as a stronghold against the Scots was made redundant when James VI of Scotland was crowned King of England, to reign as James I and so uniting the two countries. Ironically, it was only during the Jacobite rising of 1715 that the castle was used for its intended defensive role. In that year, supporters of the Catholic 'Old Pretender', James Stuart, great-grandson of James VI, captured the castle. Sadly for James, his attempt to regain the throne for the Stuart line fizzled out. Lindisfarne Castle was then recaptured by troops from Berwick.

The castle remained garrisoned during the rest of the 18th century and into the 19th. In the 1860s, gun emplacements were added to the defences, the foundations for which are still visible today. Then, in 1893, the castle was abandoned and left to fall into ruin. Fortunately, in 1901, Edward Hudson, owner of *Country Life* magazine, saw the castle while on holiday in Northumberland. Hudson, smitten by the sight, arranged to lease the castle from the Crown Estates. He cannily hired renowned architect Edward Lutyens to extensively remodel it, and had the castle changed from a Tudor fortress into a charming and comfortable Edwardian home. Hudson also commissioned a delightful cottage garden, designed by Gertrude Jekyll.

Address Holy Island, Northumberland, TD15 2SH, +44 (0)1289 389244,
www.nationaltrust.org.uk | Getting there Holy Island is only accessible at low tide, so check
the tide times at holyislandcrossingtimes.northumberland.gov.uk before attempting the
journey; paid parking at Holy Island Large Car Park | Hours Opening times vary according
to the tides so check National Trust website beforehand | Tip Learn about the history of
Holy Island, as well as what flora and fauna can be seen on the island at The Lindisfarne
Centre (www.lindisfarnecentre.org).

64 Lindisfarne Priory
Safe haven?

The Holy Island of Lindisfarne (to use its impressively long formal title) is so named because it was once the seat of Christianity in the north, and arguably all of England. In A.D. 635, Oswald, King of Northumbria, gifted Aidan, an Irish monk, the island in order to found a monastery there. This Aidan successfully did, his monastery quickly growing in wealth and influence across the region. Some time in the 670s, a monk from the Scottish Borders by the name of Cuthbert joined the monastery. Cuthbert was eventually elected Bishop of Lindisfarne in 684, just three years before his death in 687.

In 793, the peace and tranquillity of Holy Island was abruptly shattered by the first in a series of Viking raids. The *Anglo-Saxon Chronicle*, written in the ninth century, notes that, before the raids, 'dreadful forewarnings come over the land of Northumbria'. These portents included 'amazing sheets of lightning and whirlwinds', as well as 'a great famine'. Less believably, 'fiery dragons' were also seen 'flying through the sky'. And then, one day, 'heathen men destroyed God's church in Lindisfarne island by fierce robbery and slaughter'. Fun for the Vikings, but terrifying for the monks of Holy Island. Many must have wondered what they'd done to deserve such destruction. Was the raid a punishment from God?

The raids continued. In 875 the monks gave up and fled inland, taking Cuthbert's body with them. It wasn't until 1082 that the monastery was refounded, after which the structure visible today was built. The most striking aspect of the priory is the delicate rainbow arch, which would once have been a rib supporting a tower above the transept. That Lindisfarne Priory is now a ruin can't be blamed on the Vikings, however. Thanks to King Henry VIII and his Dissolution of the Monasteries in 1537, the priory was abandoned once again, this time for good.

Address Holy Island, Northumberland, TD15 2RX, www.english-heritage.org.uk | Getting there Holy Island is only accessible at low tide, so check the tide times at holyislandcrossingtimes.northumberland.gov.uk before attempting the journey; paid parking at Holy Island Large Car Park | Hours Opening times vary according to the tides so check English Heritage website beforehand | Tip The neighbouring church of St Mary the Virgin is said to be the site of St Aidan's original monastery (www.stmarysholyisland.org).

65 Pilgrim's Way

Plodging for the saint

Strictly speaking, Holy Island is only an island twice a day, at high tide. At low tide, the North Sea recedes revealing vast swathes of wet mud and sand. Low tide also makes it possible to drive over to Holy Island or, if you're more daring, walk across from the mainland. Motor vehicles must take the road, built in the mid-1950s, but walkers can take the far shorter, and satisfyingly squelchy, Pilgrim's Way, the path marked out by a series of tall poles.

The Pilgrim's Way was the route taken by pilgrims travelling to Holy Island to visit the shrine of St Cuthbert, and has therefore been in use for at least 1,300 years, if not longer. In his poem 'The Holy Island', Sir Walter Scott wrote 'Dry shod o'er sands, twice every day, The pilgrims to the shrine find way; Twice every day the waves efface, Of staves and sandalled feet the trace'. Every Easter since 1976, large groups of Christians carrying wooden crosses make the journey. Often this is the culmination of several days' walking beforehand between religious sites in northern England or the Scottish Borders. A popular route is the St Cuthbert's Way, a 62-mile walk that starts in Melrose, where Cuthbert enrolled as novice monk and ends on Holy Island, where he was bishop in later life. The route was devised in 1996 by Ron Shaw, who wrote the official guidebook.

Walking the Pilgrim's Way is fun, but it's not for the slow moving or foolhardy. It should be attempted in waterproof boots or barefoot. The route is roughly three miles in length and it's sensible to allow yourself at least two hours, leaving approximately 75 minutes before low tide time for the day (though only if the tide has receded far enough). There are two refuge boxes on the route but it's a long, cold wait for rescue should you get into trouble; the incoming tide has the disconcerting habit of flowing in *very* quickly. Locals get understandably frustrated by those who misjudge their journey and come a cropper, so don't be that person.

Address Holy Island, Northumberland, TD15 2SE | Getting there Holy Island is only accessible at low tide, so check the tide times at holyislandcrossingtimes.northumberland. gov.uk before attempting the journey; the Pilgrim's Way is on the route of the St Cuthbert's Way; paid parking at Holy Island Large Car Park | Tip Two strange vertical pillars on Guile Point can be seen from the route of the Pilgrim's Way. These Victorian structures are the Old Law Beacons, that – when lined up – show sailors a safe route into Holy Island.

66 St Cuthbert's Island
Getting away from it all

St Cuthbert is arguably the most famous of Northumberland's saints. He was probably born in A.D. 634 in Dunbar, now in the Scottish Borders but at that time in the Kingdom of Northumbria. Cuthbert was a shepherd (or possibly a warrior who guarded sheep) until a vision in A.D. 651 compelled him to enter the monastery of Melrose. There he may have stayed if not for a schism within the church. At the Synod of Whitby in A.D. 663, it was decided that the Northumbrian church would embrace Roman rather than Celtic church customs. Although Cuthbert was brought up in the Celtic tradition, he accepted the change and was appointed prior of Lindisfarne Priory (see ch. 64).

Cuthbert was by nature a solitary man. St Cuthbert's (or Hobthrush) Island is an islet just off the coast of Holy Island. Like its bigger neighbour, St Cuthbert's Island can be reached on foot at low tide. However, it is cut off *far* more quickly when the tide rises and so is a true island for longer. Local legend has it that Cuthbert withdrew there for solitary contemplation when life at the priory got too much. It's also said that the monks were able to shout across to Cuthbert, so he didn't get the peace he desired. From A.D. 676 he lived a hermit's life on Inner Farne until he was made bishop of Hexham in A.D. 684. A year later, he returned to Lindisfarne to become the priory's bishop. Whether he ever thought about his old home just across the bay isn't known.

The saint loved animals. However, he seems to have disliked women intensely. One reason given is that he was once falsely accused of fathering a child with the daughter of a Pictish king. Cuthbert prayed for a sign that this was untrue, at which the woman was swallowed up by a hole that opened up beneath her. She was only restored to the king after he promised that no woman would ever enter a church dedicated to Cuthbert.

Address Holy Island, Northumberland, TD15 2RZ | **Getting there** Both St Cuthbert's Island and Holy Island are only accessible at low tide; check the tide times at holyislandcrossingtimes.northumberland.gov.uk before attempting the journey to Holy Island; paid parking at Holy Island Large Car Park | **Tip** St Cuthbert is buried in Durham Cathedral in a touchingly simple shrine (www.durhamcathedral.co.uk).

67 __ St Mary's Well

Pilgrims welcome

The origin of the name Jesmond has a religious connection. According to legend, at some point after the Norman invasion of 1066, an apparition of the Virgin Mary, holding the infant Jesus, was seen atop a rock. This remarkable event led to the naming of the place as 'Jessemougth' or 'Jesusmound', which eventually became Jesmond.

The people of Jesmond showed their appreciation for being honoured this way by building St Mary's Chapel. Now an atmospheric ruin, in its time the chapel was a site of worship for locals and pilgrims alike. A lesser-known tribute to Mary is just off a back lane in a housing estate, hidden away in a hollow surrounded by trees. This is St Mary's Well and may well have been on the route taken by pilgrims during the medieval period, a route that included what is now Pilgrim Street in Newcastle.

Holy wells were thought to have healing properties, and were often used for baptism services. Many holy wells were co-opted pagan sites, rebadged with a saint's name to remove any heathen associations. (The throwing of coins into wells was once a way to thank the gods for providing drinking water.) There's no evidence that St Mary's Well was once a pagan place of worship. In fact, there's considerable evidence that St Mary's Well only dates back to the 17th century, long after the time when pilgrims made their way to Jesmond. The well itself was also extensively remodelled in the 19th century, so no trace of earlier structures is now visible.

It was the Reformation that effectively ended widespread worship of the Virgin Mary in England. Such Catholic practices were condemned in the new Protestant age of the Church of England, though true believers ignored repressive strictures even when threatened with execution. However, whether you're a believer or not, St Mary's Well is a wonderfully peaceful place to spend a few minutes alone in quiet contemplation.

Address The Grove, Jesmond, Newcastle upon Tyne, NE2 2ES | **Getting there** Bus 900 and Q3 Quaycity VOLTRA to Osborne Road-Acorn Road and then a short walk; limited on-street parking nearby and at the Banqueting House and then a short walk | **Tip** St George's Church is a splendid Victorian building decorated in an Arts and Crafts style (www.stgeorgesjesmond.org.uk).

68__Kielder Observatory
'Space is big'

Satellite images of Britain at night reveal the hotspots of human habitation. London is a bright splat of light; Birmingham, Liverpool and Manchester create a luminous (if wonky) triangle; and the three cities of Middlesbrough, Sunderland and Newcastle generate a cheery glowing ribbon of light. However, Britain is not uniformly illuminated. Much of Northumberland is dark, which makes the county an ideal place for astronomy.

This fact was not lost on Gary Fildes, who moved to Kielder in 2000. After hosting a series of popular 'nightwatch' events for Forestry England, Fildes established Kielder Star Camp for enthusiastic amateur astronomers. The idea of building a permanent observatory came after Fildes met Peter Sharpe, the curator of art and architecture projects for the Kielder Water and Forest Park Development Trust. A design competition was announced with the brief that the proposed observatory should complement the Kielder landscape. The winner – selected from 230 entrants – was the London-based architectural firm Charles Barclay.

Kielder Observatory was opened in March 2008 by former Astronomer Royal Sir Arnold Wolfendale, with Fildes as its first director. Over 700 public events are now held annually, though these events are so popular that places need to be booked many months in advance. Staff at the observatory are ably assisted by KOAS – the Kielder Observatory Astronomical Society – a group of cheerful volunteers who willingly give up their spare time to help out.

There are two main 'turrets' at the observatory. The 'Sir Patrick Moore' houses a 16-inch reflector telescope and a 5-inch refracting telescope. The smaller turret also has a 16-inch reflector telescope, as well as a 3.5-inch solar telescope. But perhaps the most rewarding place to be on a clear night is the Observing Deck, with the universe stretching off into infinity directly over your head.

Address Black Fell, Off Shilling Pot, Kielder, Northumberland, NE48 1EJ, +44 (0)191 2655510, www.kielderobservatory.org | Getting there Parking at the Observatory | Hours Only open during ticketed events listed on the observatory website | Tip Presentations on astronomy, spaceflight and other related subject are regularly shown at the Great North Museum's cosy planetarium (www.greatnorthmuseum.org.uk).

69_ Kielder Water
Tap into the reservoir

The Pennines, a range of hills known as the spine of England, largely protects the north east from extreme wet weather rolling in from the Atlantic. (Alas, Cumbria, on the 'wrong' side of the Pennines is not so fortunate.) This is good news for ombrophobic folk in the region but not so great for industries on Tyneside, Wearside and Teesside that need a reliable water supply. When industry boomed in the 1960s, this was a knotty problem indeed. The answer was remarkably bold and ambitious: create Europe's largest artificial lake by damming the River North Tyne west of the village of Falstone in the Kielder Valley.

A public inquiry on the proposal was first held at Newcastle's Civic Centre in 1972. Construction of Kielder Water then began in 1975, one year after parliamentary approval was granted. Building the lake was not without cost, however. The site was chosen partly for its low population density. Despite this, the hamlet of Yarrow, a school and various farms were in the way. In total 95 people were relocated elsewhere in the region. One persistent myth is that the buildings still lie beneath the water's surface. This is not the case. Were you to drain Kielder – where would you put the water? – you'd never find them. All traces of human habitation were demolished long before the valley was flooded.

Kielder Water was completed in 1981 and opened by Queen Elizabeth II the following year. The reservoir has an overall capacity of 44,000 billion gallons of water, is 170-feet deep, and has a 27-mile-long shoreline. A hydroelectric plant, powered by the outflow of water back into the River North Tyne, generates enough electricity to power a town the size of Hexham. Ironically, industry declined in the north east after Kielder Water was complete. But it does mean that northern households are unlikely to face a hosepipe ban, even in the driest of summers.

Address Hawkhope Car Park, Falstone, Northumberland, NE48 1BH, Tower Knowe Car Park, Falstone, NE 48 1BX, or Leaplish Waterside Park, Kielder, Northumberland, NE 48 1BT, www.visitkielder.com | Getting there Paid parking at the various car parks around Kielder Reservoir (a ticket bought at one car park is valid in other car parks) | Tip Ospreys can be seen nesting at Kielder during the summer months. An easier way to view raptors is to visit the Kielder Water Birds of Prey Centre, where you can see owls, hawks and even vultures (www.kielderbopc.com).

70 Killingworth Lake
Industrial wasteland made good

Modern Killingworth is a 1960s planned town that dwarfs the original village, which – thankfully – wasn't obliterated by the newer development and is now a designated conservation area. A far-sighted aspect of the Killingworth scheme was the creation in 1964 of a large lake, built on land reclaimed from the (by then) defunct Killingworth Colliery and West Moor Pit. Actually, make that two lakes: Southgate Road cuts through the eastern end of the lake, creating the effect of a drawbridge crossing over a moat. The road led directly to Killingworth Towers, a brutally modernist block of flats that was designed in 1967 to fulfil – in an are-you-sure-about-this? sort of way – the concept of a 'medieval castle-town'. The towers were demolished in 1986, but the lakes fortunately remain.

Despite being thoroughly artificial, Killingworth Lake is now a wildlife haven. Frequently seen on the lake are waterfowl such as mallard, coot and tufted duck, as well as the largest bevy of mute swans in north-east England. Anglers can fish for species such as roach and carp, as well as pike during the spring and summer months. And dragonflies are a common sight around the lake, busily darting across the water during warm weather. One reason why Killingworth Lake is so successful as a nature site was the launching of artificial islands in 2019. Made from recycled and non-toxic materials, the islands create an environment for animals and plants to live, both above and below the surface of the lake. They are also one part of a £6-million flood-prevention scheme, so making them a win-win for people and the natural world.

Killingworth Lake is now home to one of five Areas of Reflection and Contemplation in North Tyneside. These are places for people to remember those who were lost during the coronavirus pandemic. A cycle route has recently been created too, linking the lake to Silverlink Biodiversity Park, another green space in an urban area.

Address West Bailey, Killingworth, NE12 6TN, my.northtyneside.gov.uk | Getting there
Bus 62, 63 or X 63 to West Bailey – Garth 7; free parking at Lakeshore Car Park | Tip
Until 1865, Killingworth Village was in the parish of nearby Longbenton. The Church
of St John the Evangelist was built in 1869 to celebrate Killingworth Village becoming a
parish in its own right.

71 The Loraine Monument
Bloody murder

The border region was a wild and lawless place during the late Middle Ages. Rumbling hostility between England and Scotland frequently flared into brutal warfare. In this devastated land, blackhearted family clans known as Border Reivers took advantage of the chaos. For nearly 400 years, no farm or village was safe from looting by Reivers. Rustling livestock was a speciality, though they weren't averse to kidnapping for ransom either.

In a farm field near the hamlet of Kirkharle is a monument to Robert Loraine, who fell foul of a Scottish Reiver gang. According to the *Pedigree and Memoirs of the Family of Loraine of Kirkharle*, written in 1738 by M. E. Lyon, Loraine was probably born in 1451 and inherited the estate of Kirkharle 'upon the death of Edward Loraine' curiously, 'by descent', with no indication how close the relationship between the two men was. Loraine is described in Lyon's book as 'a zealous prosecutor of robbers, thieves, and moss-troopers, and for Border-Service kept a certain number of horses and arms always ready, suitable to his estate'. He was friendly with other local landowners, including the Fenwicks of Wallington, the Middletons of Belsay, and the Shaftoes of Babington. Cannily, these friendships were useful when help was needed to avenge '…the Scots' excursions and depredations into Northumberland'.

This obviously peeved the Scots to no end for they were filled 'with such malice that they resolved to have his life'. In 1483, while walking from St Wilfrid's Church, Loraine was set upon by an armed gang. They 'dragged him into an adjacent close, and there barbarously murdered him, cutting his body into small pieces to fulfil their frequent menace to "cut him as small as flesh for the pot", a ghastly testimony to the prowess of the man whose death the marauders had been unable to compass in open fight'. Loraine has been known as 'The Unfortunate Gentleman' ever since.

Address Kirkharle, Northumberland, NE19 2PE | Getting there Very limited parking near St Wilfrid's Church | Tip The nearby Kirkharle Courtyard is a community of artisan shops and independent retailers. There's also local produce on sale, as well as a coffee shop where you can buy home-cooked food. And, if you need to work off the calories, there are paths to explore around the estate (www.kirkharlecourtyard.co.uk).

72 St Wilfrid's Church
How does your garden grow?

The English can be thanked for their contribution to world culture in a number of ways. Football and cricket, for example, fish and chips, the crime novel, the sandwich, and, of course, David Attenborough. The English also created a particular style of country garden, one which, at first glance, looks thoroughly naturalistic and timeless, but that was crafted through sheer hard work and a good dollop of imagination.

The man who essentially invented the English country garden was Lancelot Brown. He was born in Kirkharle to William, a yeoman farmer, and Ursula, a chambermaid at Kirkharle Hall, probably in 1715. In 1716 he was baptised in St Wilfrid's Church, an event commemorated by a simple plaque in the nave of the church. Brown was educated at the village school in Cambo before starting an apprenticeship as a gardener's boy at the age of 14. After serving seven years, Brown left Northumberland to make a name for himself as an 'improver of grounds'. In 1741, at the age of 26, Brown joined staff of the Stowe estate in Buckinghamshire as head gardener.

Before Brown, large gardens were usually laid out in a very formal manner, with extensive use of symmetry and geometric shapes. Brown changed all that. Working as a freelance garden designer after his stint at Stowe, he created pleasingly natural gardens for his many aristocratic clients. Producing Arcadian perfection was far from easy. In one particularly busy year, Brown had over 91,000 trees planted. And, in order to create the gardens he imagined, prodigious amounts of earth would often be shifted around, with huge lakes conjured up and rivers rerouted. He quickly became known as Capability Brown for his habit of declaring that properties had 'great capabilities' before he set to work on them. Brown died in 1783, a wealthy man and one whose work we are still able to enjoy nearly 250 years on.

IN MEMORY OF
LANCELOT("CAPABILITY")BROWN
1716 ~ 1783
Baptised here 30th August 1716.
"He sought an image of Heaven".

Address Kirkharle, Northumberland, NE19 2PE | **Getting there** Very limited parking at St Wilfrid's Church | **Hours** Accessible 24 hours | **Tip** Brown returned to Northumberland in the 1760s to advise Sir Walter Blackett, owner of the Wallington estate. What Brown suggested is now unclear but it's thought that he had a hand in relocating the estate's walled garden, the design of the Owl House and the creation of the 'Low Lake' (www.nationaltrust.org.uk).

73 Clock Tower

Ding dong!

In *An Historical, Topographical, and Descriptive View of the County of Northumberland (volume 2)*, John Leland, King Henry VIII's antiquarian, is quoted as having praised Morpeth as a 'far fayrar towne then Alnwicke'. People from Morpeth shouldn't be too smug, however. The author, Eneas Mackenzie, then goes on to say that 'Alnwick must have been greatly improved since this comparison was made, or Morpeth has deteriorated'. The book was published in 1825 and a lot has happened in the two centuries since. Morpeth can hold its head high as it's a charming town, with a good number of interesting historical buildings, a wonderful green space in the shape of Carlisle Park, and a busy main shopping street.

One particularly striking building (literally and figuratively!) is the Clock Tower at the end of Oldgate. At 60 feet in height and with walls over three feet thick, it's a substantial structure. Although the tower looks medieval, the lower two-thirds were probably built early in the 17th century. It has this confusing air of antiquity because the stone it's built from was recycled, possibly from nearby Newminster Abbey, which was closed in 1537 when King Henry VIII had England's monasteries dissolved.

The top third of the tower is a belfry with six bells, added in 1706. The bells were provided by Major General Edmund Maine when he was elected MP for Morpeth in 1705. Maine did not long remain an MP as he lost his seat in 1708, and died in 1711 at the age of 78 after several years of ill health. The bells were rung at 8pm every day to signal the evening curfew. This tradition continues, though there is now no need to heed the call and head home. The bells are rung by the Morpeth Clock Tower Bellringers, who are all volunteers. The bells are also sounded during local and national events. On 19 September, 2022, muffled bells were rung for one hour before the state funeral of Queen Elizabeth II.

Address 2–4 Oldgate, Morpeth, Northumberland, NE61 1LT | Getting there Bus 2, 43, X15, X18, 417 and various others to Morpeth Bus Station; two hours free parking at Goose Hill Car Park (requires a parking disc that can be bought at the car park) | Hours Viewable from the outside only | Tip Whitehouse Farm Centre is agricultural fun for all the family. See traditional farm animals such as cows and horses, as well as more exotic beasts such as Curly Hair Tarantula (www.whitehousefarmcentre.co.uk).

74 Emily Davison's Grave
The ultimate sacrifice

It's now hard to appreciate just how few rights British women had at the turn of the 20th century. Perhaps the most egregious example was the denial of the right to vote. Women and their male supporters did not take the situation lightly, however. There were two main groups who campaigned for the right of women to vote: the suffragists and the suffragettes. Although they had the same aim, the two groups used very different strategies.

The suffragist movement essentially began in 1866. From the start, suffragists used peaceful methods to advance their cause. This included the use of petitions, the printing of posters and leaflets, and public meetings. These tactics continued with the formal union of regional suffragist groups into the National Union of Women's Suffrage in 1897. Some women, however, wanted a more active and confrontational approach. These were the suffragettes, who formed the Women's Social and Political Union in 1903. Under the leadership of Emmelinc Pankhurst, the WSPU embarked on a campaign of civil disobedience, smashing windows and resisting arrest. When imprisoned, suffragettes regularly staged hunger strikes. These often led to a force feeding by unsympathetic prison officers.

Emily Wilding Davison was one such dedicated and militant suffragette. In total, she was arrested nine times and went on hunger strike seven times for her activities. However, she is now best known for her death in support of the cause. On 4 June, 1913, Davison travelled to Epsom racecourse to attend that year's Derby. During the race she entered the course and – in a moment captured on film – attempted to grab the reins of King George V's horse, Anmer. She stood no chance and was critically injured, dying four days later having never regained consciousness. Davison was buried in the churchyard of St Mary the Virgin in Morpeth. *Deeds not words*, the motto of the WSPU, are inscribed on her gravestone.

GREATER LOVE HATH NO MAN
THAN THIS, THAT A MAN LAY
DOWN HIS LIFE FOR HIS FRIENDS
St JOHN. XV CHP XIII VERSE

EMILY WILDING
DAVISON
BORN OCT. 11th 1872
DIED JUNE 8th 1913.
DEEDS NOT WORDS.

ALFRED NORRIS
DAVISON
SON OF
C. E. DAVISON
WHO DIED AT VANCOUVER B.C.
JANUARY 26th 1918
AGED 48 YEARS.

LORD THY GOD IS WITH THEE

ERECTED
IN AFFECTIONATE MEMORY OF
SARAH SETON
THE BELOVED WIFE OF
CHARLES E. DAVISON
OF WINTON HOUSE, MORPETH
WHO DIED 30th APRIL 1866
AGED 44 YEARS.

CHARLES E. DAVISON
WHO DIED 7TH FEBRUARY 1893
AGED 70 YEARS.
AT REST

ALSO MARGARET
WIFE OF THE ABOVE
WHO DIED AT LONGHORSLEY
3RD FEBRUARY 1918

Address St Mary the Virgin, Morpeth, Northumberland, NE61 2QF | **Getting there**
Bus X14 Max, X15 Max or X18 Max to Sun Inn; train to Morpeth and then a 12-minute
walk; two hours free parking at Goose Hill Car Park and then a 13-minute walk (requires
a parking disc that can be bought at the car park) | **Tip** A statue of Davison can be seen
in Morpeth's Carlisle Park. The statue is one and a half times life size and depicts Davison
tipping out a bowl of food while on hunger strike. It was created by sculptor Ray Lonsdale
and unveiled in 2018, the centenary of the Representation of the People Act, which granted
the vote to women over 30 and who met a property qualification.

75 Northumbrian Pipes
Music to your ears

Scottish bagpipes have a smaller and sweeter-sounding cousin in the Northumbrian smallpipes. One significant difference between the two (apart from size) is the way that they're played: the bag on the Northumbrian pipes is inflated by bellows, rather than lung power as Scottish pipes are. This has the advantage that a musician can sing along to a tune as they play, arguably making the Northumbrian pipes a more sociable instrument too.

The Morpeth Chantry Bagpipe Museum is the place to go to find out more. The various pipes on display largely came from the William Alfred Cocks bagpipe collection, which was originally gifted to Newcastle's Society of Antiquaries after Cocks' death in 1971. The collection includes a set of pipes that are thought to have belonged to King Louis XIV of France, as well as pipes used during the Jacobite Rebellion.

The Northumbrian smallpipe was first developed on Tyneside in the late 18th century. One of these early pipes can be seen in the Chantry collection. They belonged to John Peacock, a professional musician from Newcastle. The pipes were made specially for Peacock in 1797 by John Dunn, the inventor of the modern instrument. Peacock was regarded as a master at the Northumbrian pipes, and was championed by the artist and engraver Thomas Bewick. In 1805, Peacock wrote *A Favourite Collection of Tunes with Variations Adapted for the Northumberland Small Pipes, Violin or Flute*, the first book of music published for the Northumbrian pipes. Sadly, despite his musicality and virtuosity on the pipes, Peacock died in poverty in 1817 at the age of 61.

The modern equivalent of Peacock is Kathryn Tickell, who has a deserved reputation as the region's foremost Northumbrian piper. Tickell has released albums with her band, and has recorded with artists such as The Chieftains and Sting.

Address The Morpeth Chantry, Bridge Street, Morpeth, Northumberland, NE61 1PD, +44 (0)1670 624490, www.museumsnorthumberland.org.uk | Getting there Bus X14 Max, X15 Max, X18 Max and various others to Damside; train to Morpeth and then a 10-minute walk; two hours free parking at Goose Hill Car Park (requires a parking disc that can be bought at the car park) | Hours Mon–Sat 9.30am–5pm | Tip The Northumbrian Pipers' Society regularly organise concerts and workshops across the region to promote the playing of the Northumbrian pipes (www.northumbrianpipers.org.uk).

76 — *Couple*
Looking out to sea

Public art can be surprisingly contentious. For example, the much-loved and iconic *Angel of the North* was roundly disparaged when first announced (see ch. 60). However, *Couple*, by sculptor Sean Henry, *really* divides opinion. It is, according to Jonathan Jones, art critic and former Turner Prize judge, the 'stupidest sculpture of the past 20 years' and one of the six worst modern public works of art in Britain. In the same spiky article for *The Guardian*, Jones also stated that it is an 'eye-wounding erection on a seashore that never did any harm to anyone' and 'totally wrecks its environment'. Residents of Newbiggin have an ambivalent attitude to the piece too, though opinion is slowly changing.

Couple was the first permanent offshore sculpture in the UK. The two figures, a middle-aged man and woman, are 16 feet high or roughly three times life-size. The painted bronze sculpture was commissioned by Inspire, the South East Northumberland Public Art and Design Initiative, and installed in 2007. It was the cherry on the cake of a £10 million coastal erosion programme. The 24-foot-high platform on which *Couple* stands is midway along a 656-foot-long stone breakwater designed to protect the wonderful sandy beach at Newbiggin.

One thing it's not possible to do is view the sculpture up close. Fortunately, *Land Couple*, handily placed on The Promenade, is a smaller version of *Couple*. Despite the reduction in scale, *Land Couple* does make it easier to see how detailed the two figures are. Both were loosely based on real people, though features were changed to make the sculpture less representative and more anonymous. Both are dressed in jeans and both are bare-armed. The paint used on *Couple* is marine paint, usually used on buoys, and developed to withstand the punishment of winter storms. Despite what Jones may hope, *Couple* is definitely staying put.

Address The Promenade, Newbiggin-by-the-Sea, Northumberland, NE64 6DB | Getting there Bus X21 Sapphire to Cresswell Arms; free parking at Church Point Car Park | Hours Viewable from the beach only | Tip The 4,200-foot-long promenade is the longest in Northumberland and is the perfect place to watch for migratory seabirds and the dolphins that visit the bay.

77 The Keelmen's Hospital
Looking after their own

A keel was a large shallow-draft sail boat that carried coal from Newcastle along the River Tyne, to colliers waiting out on the North Sea. The men who worked on them were known as keelmen, and for nearly 500 years they were the kings of the river. However, their work was brutally hard and dirty, and precariously dependent on the weather, the tides, and the supply of coal. Many keelmen either spent long periods without work or were forced to take other jobs elsewhere on the river. It was a life only suited to young men too; very few keelmen were able to work beyond the age of 50.

What set the keelmen apart was their sense of community. The evidence for this is found in the handsome shape of the Keelmen's Hospital in Newcastle, as it was paid for by the keelmen themselves. Completed in 1701, the hospital cost £2,000 to build. This (then sizeable) sum was met by a contribution of a penny a tide from a crew's wages. The hospital was used as an almshouse for sick or ageing keelmen, or their widows and children.

The age of the keelmen essentially came to an end just 50 years after the hospital was built. The construction of waggonways made it easier to transport coal long distances overland. Wooden staiths, such as the wonderfully preserved example at Dunston, were also built on the Tyne. These often-huge structures were used to load colliers directly with coal, bypassing the need for keels. The keelmen came out on strike in 1794 in protest but to little effect. The invention of the steam tug in the 19th century was the final straw. The number of keels on the river gradually declined, until they had all gone by the 1890s.

Controversially, the Keelmen's Hospital has been allowed to decay since 2009, when it ceased in its modern role as student accommodation. To let it deteriorate further would be a gross failure to honour the men who helped make Newcastle what it is.

Address City Road, Newcastle upon Tyne, NE1 2AB | Getting there Bus Q3 Quaycity VOLTRA to City Road-Gibson Street; Metro to Manors (Yellow line) and then a short walk; paid parking at St Ann's Car Park | Hours Viewable from the outside only | Tip Dunston Staiths is thought to be the largest timber structure in Europe (www.dunstonstaiths.org.uk).

78 Lantern Tower
Crowning achievement

There has been a church on the site of Newcastle Cathedral (more formally, the Cathedral Church of St Nicholas) since the 11th century, just a short walk from the 'new' castle that gives the city its name. However, thanks to a fire in 1216, not much of the original church still survives. The building seen today largely dates from 1350, with the notable exception of the distinctive lantern tower, work on which began in 1448.

Newcastle was a rich city during the medieval period, and its wealthy merchants contributed large sums of money for the upkeep of its churches. The addition of the lantern tower to St Nicholas' was paid for by Robert Rhodes, a successful lawyer and mayor of Newcastle from 1429–31. His reward – other than increasing his chance of eternal salvation – was the addition of his coat of arms to the cathedral's handsome marble font.

The lantern tower is an unusual feature for an English church, and was the first of its kind in the country. Although charmingly decorative, the tower once had the eminently useful function as a navigation beacon for ships sailing up the River Tyne. At just over 190 feet in height, the tower was, for centuries, the tallest structure in Newcastle and so would have been easily seen from some distance away.

The tower has had its problems, however. In 1644, during the English Civil War, a Scottish army besieged Newcastle. Legend has it that Newcastle's mayor, Sir John Marlay, moved Scottish prisoners to the tower to discourage the invaders from destroying it. In 1832 it was discovered that the tower was starting to lean. This was partially solved by the addition of substantial stone porches on the north and south sides of the tower. And then, in 1868, the foundations were reinforced with concrete. Ironically, on 1 April, 1801, the *London Courier* mischievously reported that the tower *had* collapsed, an April Fool's joke that may have come horribly true.

Address St Nicholas Square, Newcastle upon Tyne, NE1 1PF, www.newcastlecathedral.org.uk |
Getting there Bus 27 Crusader, 56 Cityrider, 57 and various others to High Level Bridge
North End | Hours Mon–Fri 7.30am–6pm, Sat 8am–4pm, Sun 7.30am–6pm; during the
summer months there are regular tours to the top of the lantern tower (see the cathedral
website for more details) | Tip St Andrew's is the oldest church in Newcastle, with parts
dating back to the 12th century. A short section of the now largely demolished old city wall
can also be seen at the west end of the graveyard (www.standrewsnewcastle.org.uk).

79 St Mary's Church
Flatpacked

There are plenty of churches built from stone or brick in Northumberland. St Mary's Church in Newton-by-the-Sea is a quirky exception. The church is a 'Tin Tabernacle', made of corrugated galvanised iron. 'Tin tabernacles' were a Victorian invention and were usually meant to be temporary structures prior to the building of a more permanent church. They were ordered from catalogues and would arrive in 'flatpack' form for assembly on site.

The need for 'Tin Tabernacles' largely arose due to the rapid increase in population during the 19th century, though it's hard to imagine teeming hordes in Newton-by-the-Sea. They were cheap to buy and easy to repair, making them ideal for placing in poorer areas. Despite their functional appearance, many 'Tin Tabernacles' had gothic embellishments and were highly decorated inside.

Corrugated iron was invented by Henry Robinson Palmer who, in 1829, took out a patent for 'indented or corrugated metallic sheets'. Initially, Palmer's invention was used to build warehousing in London Dockland, the Turpentine Shed being the first building in the world with a corrugated iron roof. Unfortunately, corrugated iron had its detractors. In 1890, William Morris, a leading figure in the Arts and Crafts movement, protested at the way that the material was 'now spreading like a pestilence over the country'.

St Mary's was built to be used as a Mission Room sometime in the 1890s. In 1902, a licence was granted so that Holy Communion and baptism services could be held in the church. On 12 December, 1903, a James Richard Carss was the first child to be baptised at St Mary's. Although corrugated galvanised iron is a durable material, it does not last for ever. (Galvanising is the process of dipping iron into tin or zinc to prevent corrosion.) In 1994, St Mary's was reroofed with new steel sheeting, making it ready for another century of use.

Address Newton-by-the-Sea, Northumberland, NE66 3HW, www.stmaryschurch.info |
Getting there Paid parking at Low Newton Car Park | Hours Viewable from the outside
only except during services or open days | Tip The Ship Inn is a small but atmospheric
pub with its own micro-brewery. The food served at lunchtime is fresh and locally sourced,
including crab and kippers (www.shipinnnewton.co.uk).

80 Agricultural Shows
All the fun of the fair

Northumberland is a largely rural county so it's no surprise that agricultural shows are a big part of the yearly calendar of events. By far the largest is the Northumberland County Show, held at Bywell every Spring Bank Holiday. This show attracts over 23,000 people, who go to enjoy the sheep-shearing demonstrations, Cumberland wrestling, fairground rides, and to eat beef burgers and doughnuts, drink beer, and buy handmade items from local artists.

There is also keenly fought competition between farmers for who has the best sheep, cattle, horses, pigs, rabbits, poultry and goats in the county, with coveted 'First Prize' rosettes awarded to the winning animals. Locals also compete for prizes in the Home Crafts marquee, in categories such as Lemon Drizzle Cake, Tea Cosy, Royal Memorabilia and Painting (Any Medium). The show is *not* a white-knuckle ride of excitement, but it's a thoroughly fun and enjoyable event for all the family.

The other shows in Northumberland are far smaller but no less pleasurable, and each has its own particular character. The Bellingham Show boasts the wittily named Reivers Return beer tent, with live music from local acts on hand all day to entertain visitors. And the Harbottle Show, which was first held in 1862, features terrier racing and wellie flinging competitions.

The last show in the season is the Alwinton Border Shepherds' Show, held early in October. As the name suggests, the show is biased towards sheep and sheep farming. One breed regularly seen at the show is the Cheviot, a hardy white-faced sheep named after the range of hills that loom over Alwinton. The hills also provide the setting for the show's fell race, open to both adults and children. The course is roughly three miles in length and starts and finishes on the show field. Eating beef burgers and doughnuts beforehand isn't recommended, though.

Address At various locations across Northumberland, www.northcountyshow.co.uk, www.harbottleshow.com, www.bellinghamshow.co.uk, www.alwintonshow.co.uk | Getting there Parking in a designated area set aside by the event organiser | Hours See show websites for details | Tip Ouseburn Farm is a working farm in urban Newcastle that aims to teach children about caring for animals in an educational but fun environment (www.ouseburnfarm.org.uk).

81   Black Middens

Not made of sticks or straw but stone

Castles are found all across the UK, but the bastle is unique to the Border region of England and Scotland. A bastle is a fortified farmhouse, sturdily built from stone with walls many feet thick. They typically date from the 16th century, when north Northumberland was a lawless place thanks to the Border Reivers.

Bastles were solidly built to keep farmers and their families safe during frequent Reiver raids. Reivers usually stole livestock, making them precursors of cattle rustlers in the American Wild West. Bastles were two storeys high, with valuable animals kept on the ground floor when danger threatened. The owners lived on the upper floor of the bastle. This was accessed by a ladder that could be pulled up at night or during a raid. Windows were generally small, which increased the strength of the structure but would have provided very little light or ventilation.

The word bastle derives from the French 'bastille', which is a stronghold typically used as a prison. Bastles weren't prisons, though they may have felt like one as the frightened occupants cowered inside waiting for a raid to end. Black Middens near Greenhaugh is a slightly atypical bastle as it has an exterior stone staircase leading to the upper doorway.

Black Middens was attacked at least once during its history. In 1583, Kinmont Willie Armstrong and his gang killed six people and stole livestock in a bloody raid on the bastle and seven other farmsteads nearby. An external staircase therefore makes no sense. After all, why make life easier for men intent on larceny? The answer is that the era of the Border Reivers effectively ended in 1603, when King James VI of Scotland was crowned King James I of England. Anglo-Scottish rivalries subsided and law and order gained the upper hand. The staircase was therefore added later, when comfort and convenience finally trumped safety and security.

Address Near Greenhaugh, Northumberland, NE48 1NE,
www.northumberlandnationalpark.org.uk, www.english-heritage.org.uk | Getting there
Free car park nearby and then a short walk | Hours Open during daylight hours | Tip
Woodhouses Bastle House near Holystone is a more complete example than Black
Middens and can be viewed from inside on guided tour days during the summer
months (www.northumberlandnationalpark.org.uk).

82 Bremenium
Lonely outpost

Commissioned in A.D. 122, Hadrian's Wall consolidated the north-western boundary of the Roman Empire. There are, however, substantial and important Roman sites that were built *before* Hadrian's Wall and much further north too. One of these sites is Bremenium (or High Rochester) Fort.

Bremenium was built around A.D. 80 during a Roman campaign against native tribes in what is now Northumberland and the Scottish Borders. The campaign was led by Gnaeus Julius Agricola, who, in A.D. 78, had been made the first governor of Britain. Obviously keen to stamp his authority, Agricola had already conquered Anglesey before turning his attention to northern Britain.

To keep troops and supplies moving, Agricola had a road built from Eboracum (York) into the Scottish Borders to Melrose (and even possibly as far as Dalkeith). This road later came to be known as Dere Street, after Deira, the Anglo-Saxon word for Yorkshire. The Roman name for the road – if it even had a name – is now completely lost to history.

Bremenium was one of a number of forts built along Dere Street to protect the road. During its operational use the fort was rebuilt at least twice. It was heavily fortified, with thick stone walls and with platforms to support *onagri*, a catapult for firing stone missiles. This is an indication of its precarious position north of Hadrian's Wall. For 200 years Bremenium was the most northerly outpost of the Roman Empire, so the soldiers would have appreciated the fort's sheer solidity. Not much now remains of the Bremenium, other than a few stretches of wall and entrance gates, the best preserved of which is the western gate. Much of the stone was removed (or, less politely, plundered) over the years to build local cottages and farmhouses. A permissible path can be followed around the fort, which is the ideal way to appreciate its original size and shape.

Address Rochester, Northumberland, NE19 1RA, www.northumberlandnationalpark.org.uk |
Getting there Limited on-street parking in Rochester and then a 15-minute walk | Hours
Viewable from the outside only | Tip The Camien Café in Rochester is the 'Last Café in
England'. Head north along the A 68 and the next chance of refreshment is in the Scottish
Borders. The café is family run and serves home-made food, as well and hot and cold drinks.

83 Catcleugh Blackhouse
Off to work we go

Kielder Water (see ch. 69) isn't the only reservoir in Northumberland. Catcleugh Reservoir is one of a chain of reservoirs that includes, Hallington, Whittle Dene, Colt Crag and Little Swinburne, all fed by water from the River Rede and connected by a series of tunnels and aqueducts. Catcleugh was built by the Newcastle and Gateshead Water Company between 1893 and 1903. Industry on Tyneside boomed during this period and the urban population rapidly increased as a result. Catcleugh and its associated reservoirs were needed to supply fresh water to Newcastle and Gateshead to meet the ever-growing demand.

Building Catcleugh was a difficult undertaking. The proposed site was remote and there was no modern road nearby to transport men and materials to the area. The solution was a 16-mile narrow gauge railway, built to connect Catcleugh to West Woodburn Station and the main railway network. Temporary wooden housing was also built on-site for the 600 workers and their families. The single-storey accommodation huts were built on both sides of the River Rede and – perhaps inevitably – the northern site was nicknamed 'Newcastle' and the southern site 'Gateshead'. Life was tough for the men and their families. The huts had no running water or electricity supply. Each room had a coal fire, the only source of heat, and paraffin lamps provided the only lighting at night.

Only one hut – the Catcleugh Blackhouse – now remains. When the reservoir was finished the 'towns' were torn down. However, the Blackhouse was kept and used as a store until the 1960s, when it was finally abandoned. By the 1980s it was in a sorry state until a local campaign persuaded the Northumberland National Park and Northumbria Water to fully restore it. Now the building is filled with fascinating historical artefacts that tell the full story of the workers and the reservoir they built.

Address Near Cleugh Manor, Byrness, Northumberland, NE19 1TS, www.northumberlandnationalpark.org.uk | **Getting there** Bus 131, 815 or 885 to Byrness Hotel and then a 25-minute walk along the A 68 (this is a fast, busy road so not really advisable); parking at Catcleugh Blackhouse | **Hours** Only viewable on official tours run by the Northumberland National Park during the summer months – see the website for details | **Tip** The Percy Cross, found in a small plantation west of Otterburn, commemorates the Battle of Otterburn, fought in 1388 between the armies of England and Scotland.

84 Cheviot
None higher

Northumberland has plenty of hills, though none could be described as lofty. Cheviot is highest, topping out at 2,674 feet above sea level. However, if Cheviot were somehow dropped into the Lake District it would only be the 13th highest peak. Cheviot wouldn't qualify as a Scottish Munro either, being below 3,000 foot in height. It *is* a Nuttall, though, which is an English or Welsh hill over 2,000 feet. So that's something. Climbing Cheviot can be a bit of a disappointment too. The summit is a long plateau dominated by peat quagmires that are wet and treacherous. Fortunately, a paved path curves its way through the bog to a disappointingly unlovely trig point.

Cheviot, and the other hills in the Cheviot range, were once far more dramatically imposing, for they are all that now remain of an extinct volcano. Approximately 400 million years ago, two continental plates slowly collided, joining what would become Scotland to prehistoric England. This caused great quantities of magma to build up below where the Cheviots now stand. At some point the pressure was released by a violent outpouring of lava. When the volcano formed, it may have been some 10,000 feet high and 37 miles wide. Since then the remorseless erosion of rain, wind and ice has reduced the Cheviots to mere nubs.

Clues to the geological history of the area are easily found. The Cheviot valleys – such as the Harthope, College and Breamish – are volcanic fault lines. Other distinctive features are tors, such as Housey Crags, Langlee Crags and Cunyan Crags, that erupt out of the landscape like broken teeth. These are outcrops of volcanic andesite that were left isolated as softer rock was eroded around them. Although slower geological processes still continue (it still rains in Northumberland, after all…), Cheviot is now a quiescent giant, even if it's a small giant as these things go.

Address Langleeford, Northumberland, NE71 6RG,
www.northumberlandnationalpark.org.uk | **Getting there** Parking at Langleeford in the
Harthope Valley and then a two to three hour walk to the summit of Cheviot | **Tip** A
particularly challenging walk is the Cheviot Horseshoe. This is a 9.5-mile circular walk that
takes in Cheviot, Cairn Hill and Hedgehope Hill, the first, second and third highest peak in
the Cheviot range, respectively (and all of which are Nuttalls).

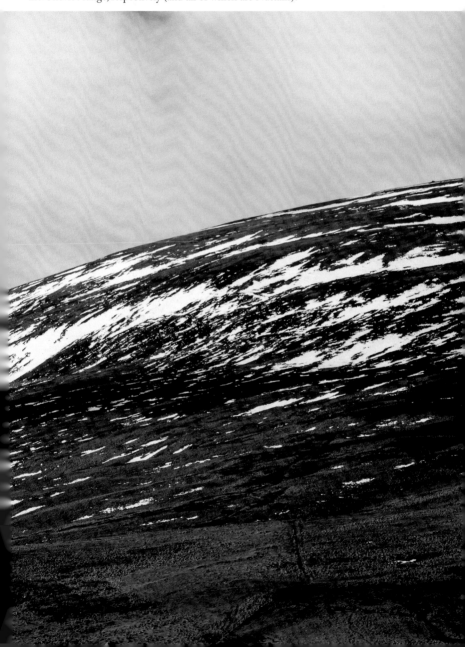

85 Clennell Street

Take the high road

The ability to whizz from A to B by car or train is something we modern Britons take for granted. However, it's really not so very long ago in the scheme of things that long journeys went at a far slower pace; you either walked to your destination or – if you were one of the lucky ones – you rode on a horse or pony. Many ancient routes used by our ancestors still exist, marked on maps as footpaths and now walked purely for pleasure. One of these routes is Clennell Street, which was once an important road that linked Morpeth in Northumberland and Kelso in the Scottish Borders.

People in the pre-industrial era didn't travel for the fun of it. They *really* needed a good reason to leave home, particularly if the journey involved crossing as lawless and uncivilised a region as the Cheviots. Clennell Street was largely used by drovers, moving cattle or sheep to market. This would be a slow process. A drover and his livestock would be lucky to cover 12 – 15 miles a day on the flat and probably far less on the hillier stretches of the route. Staying in control of a large herd of animals would have its frustrations too. One clever solution to this problem can still be seen approximately one mile north of the village of Alwinton. The Clennell Street Cross Dyke forced the herd to spread out in a longer line and so reduced the risk of individuals wandering merrily off on their own down the steep slope on either side.

The fact that you don't meet dozens of cattle on Clennell Street now is largely due to the invention of the railway. Trains could be used to transport animals far more quickly across longer distances and in greater numbers than a drover could manage. By the mid-19th century, the need to drove cattle and sheep began to diminish. Animals are now transported across country in a far less romantic way, in complete silence, boxed up, wrapped in cellophane and refrigerated.

Address Alwinton, NE65 7BQ, Northumberland, www.northumberlandnationalpark.org.uk | **Getting there** Clennell Street is now a bridleway from Alwinton to Uswayford and over the Scottish Border at Cocklawfoot; paid parking at the Northumberland National Park Car Park at Alwinton | **Tip** The Rose and Thistle is Alwinton's one and only pub, offering a range of hot and cold food as well as bed and breakfast (www.theroseandthistle.net).

86 Cottonshopeburnfoot
What's in a name?

The town of Llanfairpwllgwyngyllgogerychwyrndrobwllllantysili-
ogogogoch boasts the longest single-word place name in Britain.
It's also the longest single-word place name in Europe and the
second longest in the world. But it's in Wales, and this is a book
about Northumberland. Fortunately, the county has its own record-
breaker in the shape of Cottonshopeburnfoot, which is the longest
single-word place name in England. Or is it? Some sources prefer
Cottonshopeburn Foot and this would allow Blakehopeburnhaugh to
take the crown. Happily, barely a mile separates the two, so Northumberland would hold on to the record regardless. Ironically – despite
their lengthy monikers – both locations are small hamlets that are
all too easy to pass without noticing.

There is a satisfying number of places in Northumberland with
a quirky name. Unthank, of which there are two in the county, is
particularly odd. One possible reason for the strange appellation is
that it dates to a time when people lived in those places without the
consent of the local landowner, and so showed no gratitude to anyone whatsoever. Or paid rent. The scamps. Today, the name is more
commonly associated with Tyneside-born folk singers Rachel and
Becky Unthank, who, with other musicians, perform as the critically
acclaimed The Unthanks.

Then there are Ogle, Snitter, Sheepwash and Cambois. The latter odd as it's pronounced 'camuss'. Oh, and Ulgham isn't 'ulgam',
it's 'uffam'. Alnwick and Alnmouth are named after the River Aln,
which flows through both towns. When pronouncing Alnmouth you
vocalise the *l*, just as you do for the river (think Alan, but without the
second *a*). However, the *l* is dropped for Alnwick, so Ann-ick. Confusingly though, Anick, a hamlet near Hexham, is pronounced with
a different *a* sound, the same as that at the start of 'able'. It's enough
to give you Hartburn…

Address Near Rochester, Northumberland, NE19 1TF | Getting there Bus 815 and 885 to Cottonshopeburnfoot and then a short walk along a farm track to Cottonshopeburnfoot or a 25-minute walk to Blakehopeburnhaugh | Tip The Three Kings Stone Circle is one of Northumberland's relatively few stone circles (see ch. 46). The name is thought to derive from the legend that three warrior kings from Denmark were buried there (follow path off the Pennine Way near the Border Forest Holiday Park).

87 The Drake Stone
Duck tales

The quirkily named Drake Stone on the moor above Harbottle is the largest free-standing boulder in the county. Made of sandstone, weighing an impressive 2,200 tons and standing 30 feet high, it's an impressive natural feature and a local landmark. The stone is an erratic, which means that it was moved to its present position by a glacier during a recent Ice Age.

The origin of the name is something of a mystery. Drake may relate to 'draco', Latin for dragon. Or, it may be named after Sir Francis Drake due to its vague resemblance to an Elizabethan galleon, with some squinting and a lot of imagination, it has to be said. Another theory is that the stone was originally the Draag Stone, that name given to it by druids in pre-Roman Northumberland.

There are a number of myths and legends associated with the Drake Stone. One story is that voices can occasionally be heard emanating from its depths. Another is that those who spend the night nearby will be unable to leave in the morning. They are not to be confused with those who merely get stuck after climbing the stone, only to discover that getting down again is somewhat trickier.

The Drake Stone was once thought to have healing powers too, with sick children passed up and over the stone to effect a cure for their ailments. This is a far better fate than that described by John Murray in his 1864 book *A Handbook for Travellers in Durham and Northumberland*. According to Murray, the practice was 'a relic of druidical times, when they were probably passed through the fire on the same spot'. There is, of course, no evidence whatsoever that the Drake Stone could revolutionise paediatric practice. However, William Tomlinson did note in his 1889 book *Comprehensive Guide to the County of Northumberland* that 'Harbottle is an exceptionally healthy place', and that 'mortality among the children almost unknown'. So, who knows.

Address Harbottle, Northumberland, NE65 7BB, www.northumberlandnationalpark.org.uk |
Getting there Free parking at the Forestry Commission West Wood car park and then
a 30-minute walk following a path uphill across moorland | **Tip** The ruined Harbottle
Castle was once a stronghold built under the orders of Henry II. It overlooked Clennell
Street (see ch. 85) and was probably built to defend against incursion of the Scots into
Northumberland (www.northumberlandnationalpark.org.uk).

88 Great Hetha
Defensive position

A good number of hills in north Northumberland share a secret hiding in plain sight: an Iron Age hill fort, built between 800 B.C. and A.D. 43, the year of the Roman invasion of Britain. What may look at first sight like a very rough-and-ready and vaguely circular low wall of loose rock is all that now remains of these once impressive structures. One of the finest of Northumberland's many hill forts is Great Hetha at the northern end of the College Valley.

Hill forts were shared either by a tribe or, in smaller examples, an extended family. There was typically an outer ring of earthworks, usually made up of ditches and banked ramparts. Inside this enclosure would be a wooden palisade with a single (and strong) timber gate. A survey by English Heritage in 2000 found evidence that Great Hetha was developed in three separate phases. An outer enclosure was built during the first phase, which was replaced by a slightly smaller, but presumably more substantial, enclosure during the second. An inner rampart was then created during the third and final phase. Quarry sites were also identified nearby as the probable source of the stone used to build the enclosures. The survey also identified the site of at least nine huts within Great Hetha's walls. These huts would have been built from timber and probably topped off with a conical thatched roof.

The steep walk up to the top of Great Hetha indicates how defensible a spot it must have been. Also noteworthy is the splendid view in every direction, making a sneak attack more difficult. The fort is also relatively close to the College Burn, which would have provided a useful supply of fresh water. However, although Great Hetha was a stronghold, conflict was not necessarily a constant. The inhabitants of Northumberland's hill forts would have actively traded with each other, and possibly even met for religious festivals and to hunt co-operatively.

Address Near Hethpool, Northumberland, NE71 6TW | **Getting there** Free parking at the Northumberland National Park Car Park at Hethpool and then a 45-minute walk | **Tip** North of Greta Hetha is Little Hetha, another of Northumberland's hill forts. Though there is less to see than on Great Hetha, this is an easier and less strenuous site to visit.

89 Lordenshaws

Neolithic emojis?

Ancient Britons left their mark on the Northumbrian landscape in the form of cup-and-ring marked rocks. These are large – usually flat – rocks into which have been carved intricate nested circles, hollows and geometric shapes. One of the finest examples of a cup-and-ring marked rock can be found on Garleigh Moor near the remains of Lordenshaws Iron Age hillfort. The location is spectacular, overlooked by the craggy Simonside Hills and with the Cheviots (see ch. 84) visible in the far distance. If ever there was a place for a pre-historic art-form it is here.

The cup-and-ring marks were made during the Neolithic and Early Bronze Age periods, some 3,500 to 6,000 years ago. (It's sobering to think that the markings were already millennia old when the Romans invaded Britain in A.D. 43.) One puzzle is what the markings represent. A plausible hypothesis is that they were religious in nature, messages to either long-forgotten gods or local spirits, or to the recently departed. Another is that the carvings represent a form of control over the landscape, with the cups and rings mimicking the patterns and forms found in nature.

The rocks selected for carving were largely sandstone, which is easily worked. The tools used would have been made from andesite or whinstone, both hard igneous rocks. The techniques used to work the markings have been described as a mixture of 'picking' and 'pecking', using broad 'chisels' for larger symbols and finer pointed tools to create smaller details.

The greatest advocate for the glory of cup-and-ring marked rocks has to be Dr Stan Beckensall. Since the 1960s, Beckensall has carefully studied and documented over 1,500 examples across Britain and in his home county of Northumberland. That he was made an MBE in 2019 for services to Prehistoric Rock Art and History in Britain was a mystery to no one.

Address Near Rothbury, Northumberland, NE46 1BS | Getting there Free car park off the single-track Simonside road and then a short walk | Tip It's just a short walk from the cup-and-ring marked rock to Lordenshaws hillfort. The outer circular rampart and ditch of the hillfort is still clearly visible, as are the impressions of several roundhouses inside.

90 — The Motte
Not a hill

When is a door not a door? When it's ajar. It's not the funniest of jokes, but it's more mirthsome than: When is a hill not a hill? When it's a motte. You'd be forgiven for thinking that the Motte in Elsdon is a hill, though. It has all the characteristics of a hill, including slopes that go both up and down (depending on where you stand, of course…), as well as a view from the (admittedly low) summit. However, the Motte isn't a hill. Or least not a natural one.

The Motte is the site of a motte and bailey castle, built by Robert de Umfraville after the Norman Conquest of 1066. Motte and bailey castles were the forerunners of the later (and far more substantial) stone castles built by the Normans. The bailey was a courtyard within which were barracks for the soldiers of the castle, kitchens and workshops. A deep ditch and tall wooden fence (or palisade) provided protection, and the only way into the bailey was via a drawbridge and main gate. The motte was a large mound, upon which sat a wooden keep. Often the motte was built by piling vast amounts of earth into a flattened cone shape – which is what was done at Elsdon – but the Normans also used natural landscape features if they were suitable.

There are no original motte and bailey castles still standing. Wood doesn't last, which is why stone was the later building material of choice. However, motte and bailey castles were quick to build, which was a useful attribute in the early years of the Norman Conquest. The motte at Elsdon survived because the castle was abandoned some time after 1157. It was replaced by Harbottle Castle further up the Coquet Valley. This new (stone) castle was in a more useful place to protect a route through the Cheviots into Scotland. As the motte was never built upon it, it retained its original size and shape, with only centuries of Northumbrian weather softening its outline.

Address Elsdon, Northumberland, NE19 1AB | Getting there Free car park opposite
Elsdon Village Hall and then a short walk | Tip An old pinfold or sheep enclosure still
stands on Elsdon's village green. The 40-foot-wide structure probably dates from the
18th century, and was used to hold stray animals.

91 Otterburn Ranges
On manoeuvres

Some 23 per cent of the Northumberland National Park is taken up by the Otterburn Training Area, owned by the Ministry of Defence. The OTA came into existence in 1911, when land was purchased to provide an artillery range and camp for the Territorial Army (created a mere three years earlier and then known as the Territorial Force). The size of the OTA increased during World War II and has been gradually added to in the decades since.

Today, the OTA is roughly 58,000 acres in size and, out of 10 regional training areas in the UK, is one of only two where the British Army can train using modern artillery systems. Live firing takes place virtually all year round, with the notable exceptions of two weeks at Christmas and four weeks from mid-April to mid-May. Wonderfully, this latter break takes account of lambing season, for there are a number of sheep farms within the OTA.

For safety reasons, the public is not allowed onto the Controlled Access area of the OTA during firing and training days. Two beneficiaries of this restriction on public access are the local flora and fauna. The OTA boasts England's more northerly upland heath, which is home to ground-nesting birds such as black grouse and curlew, the latter used to represent the Northumberland National Park. There are also approximately 640 acres of blanket bog – a rare habitat internationally, never mind in the UK – as well as areas of ancient deciduous woodland. For these reasons, the planning of military exercises also involves taking into account the potential environmental impact.

The Open Access areas of the OTA can be freely visited all year round. Slightly disconcertingly this can mean sharing the space with soldiers in training. However, troops in the Open Access area do not fire live rounds. Only the occasional pop and flash of pyrotechnics is likely to break the silence of the hills around you.

Address Otterburn Camp, Northumberland, NE19 1NX, www.northumberlandnationalpark.org.uk | Getting there There are roads and paths leading into the OTA from the A 68 and B 6341 | Hours Access is restricted during live firing, indicated by the flying of red flags or the lighting of red lamps next to roads and paths leading into the OTA; firing times can found on www.gov.uk | Tip The outline of a Roman encampment can be seen at Chew Green, nine miles west of the village of Alwinton. Chew Green was on the route of Dere Street, a Roman road that linked York and what is now the Scottish Borders region.

92 __ The Pennine Way

'I get all me pleasure the hard moorland way'

The USA's Appalachian Trail (or AT) is a 2,200-mile walking route from Maine to Georgia, passing through 12 other states along the way. By comparison, a mere 600 miles separates the very tip of northern Scotland and the English south coast. In Britain, if you try to walk the same distance as the AT, and insist on walking in a straight line, you'll eventually fall off a cliff. However, Britons should be grateful to the AT, for it inspired the creation of the country's first long-distance national trail.

The 1930s were not a good time for those who longed to hike across Britain's wild spaces. Landowners jealously guarded the right of access to their property and the prosecution of ramblers was common ('Think of the grouse', cries an irate gamekeeper in Ewan MacColl's protest song 'The Manchester Rambler'). A mass trespass of Kinder Scout in the Peak District on 24 April, 1932 highlighted the need for the right to roam. And then, in 1935, journalist Tom Stephenson wrote an article for the *Daily Herald* entitled 'Wanted – A Long Green Trail'. The piece called for the creation of 'a Pennine Way from the Peak to the Cheviots', citing the AT as a useful model to follow. The catchy name stuck and, although it took 30 years of hard work and often bitter negotiation, the Pennine Way officially opened on 24 April, 1965, fittingly, exactly 33 years after the Kinder Scout protest.

As the name suggests, the 268-mile route of the Pennine Way follows the Pennines, from the Peak District to the Scottish Borders. The Northumberland stretch cuts across Hadrian's Wall to Bellingham, and from there through Redesdale to Byrness. The final 27-mile stretch, over the Cheviots, is the longest without habitation on the entire route. The walk then ends just over the border in Kirk Yetholm. You'd still have 1,900 miles to go to complete the AT, but finishing the Pennine Way is an achievement nevertheless.

Address Northumberland National Park, www.northumberlandnationalpark.org.uk or www.nationaltrail.co.uk | **Getting there** Bus AD 122 during the summer months to join the Pennine Way near Hadrian's Wall or Bus 815 and 885 to Cottonshopeburnfoot and then a short walk along a farm track to join the Cheviot stretch of the Pennine Way | **Tip** Several long-distance trails cross through Northumberland. The St Cuthbert's Way and St Oswald's Way both pay tribute to local saints and the places they lived in and knew.

93 The Shepherds' Cairn

A community comes together

On 16 November, 1962 a gale force wind blew in from the north. Across the country the temperatures plummeted and snow began to fall. In the Cheviots, conditions were truly grim. Driven by the wind, the snow was whipped into a blizzard. And so it continued overnight and the following day. At times the wind reached 70 miles per hour and visibility was a few inches at most.

John 'Jock' Scott, William 'Willie' Middlemas and William Bulloch were heading home from Rothbury Mart, where Jock had sold sheep. After dropping William off in Alnham, Jock and Willie continued on towards Jock's farm at Ewartly Shank, having refused an offer of beds for the night. A modern tarmac road now snakes its way over the wild moorland between Alnham and the remote farm, but, in 1962, there was only a track.

On 19 November, William Bulloch made his way to Ewartly Shank where he spoke to Margaret Scott, Jock's wife. She asked about Jock and Willie and when William thought they'd be home. Concerned, William dashed back to raise the alarm. Local farmers and shepherds joined with the police and RAF personnel to form a search party. Sadly, on 20 November, the searchers found Jock's body near High Knowes, covered in snow. Willie's body was found a few days later, just 100 yards from where Jock had been found.

An auction in aid of the 'Shepherd Disaster Fund' was held the following month. Farmers and locals donated livestock, and gifts such as fruit cakes and walking sticks. *The Journal* reported that 'After three hours of the briskest bidding ever seen there it was announced that more than £1,300 had been raised'. Eventually the fund reached £2,402 – a *very* large sum in 1962 – which went to Margaret and her two children, Carol and Thomas (Willie had no dependants). A cairn now stands near where Jock and Willie died, a poignant reminder of a tragic winter's tale.

DEDICATED
IN MEMORY OF
THE SHEPHERDS
JOCK SCOTT·WILLIE MIDDLEMAS
WHO PERISHED HERE IN THE SNOW
17TH NOVEMBER 1962

ERECTED BY
NORTHUMBERLAND NATIONAL PARK AUTHORITY
AND N.N.P. MOUNTAIN RESCUE TEAM

Address Near Alnham, Northumberland, NE66 4UF,
www.northumberlandnationalpark.org.uk | Getting there Off-road parking on
Ewartly Shank road and then a short walk | Tip The charming Church of St Michael
in Alnham dates back to the 13th century and was built on a Roman camp site.

94__ Totem Poles
Wild west (Northumberland)

The village of Stonehaugh was purpose built in 1957 to house Forestry Commission workers, employed to manage the surrounding Wark Forest at the southern end of Kielder Forest. The original plan to build 200 houses, a church, pub and school was quickly scaled back, and ultimately only 35 houses, a village hall and social club were built, with one house operating part time as the village Post Office. However, what Stonehaugh lacks in size and amenities, it more than makes up for with three magnificent and unique wooden totem poles next to its picnic area.

There have been four sets of three poles since the first set was erected in 1971. These were created by villagers Joe Potts and Allan Hutchinson to amuse Stonehaugh's children. They did more than this, however, quickly becoming a popular attraction and bringing tourists to the relatively remote village. Joe and Allan used chainsaws to create the poles, at a time when chainsaws were (literally and figuratively) cutting-edge technology. Time and the Northumbrian weather gradually took their toll on these pioneering poles, and so they were replaced in 1982 after the bases had rotted dangerously. Another Potts, Joe's brother Jimmy, created the new poles, and then again when set number three was required in 1992.

The fourth set was erected in November 2019 to celebrate the centenary of the Forestry Commission and the 70th anniversary of the UK's National Parks. The new poles are made from larch wood donated by Forestry England, and were carved by Simon Jackson, the son of a local forester and a professional chainsaw artist with more than 25 years' experience. Each pole is unique. The first has a traditional Native American motif, the second was designed by children at Wark Primary School, and the third depicts animals found in Northumberland. To stop their bases decaying, the poles have been inserted into buried water mains piping.

Address Stonehaugh, Wark, Northumberland, NE48 3DY, www.northumberlandnationalpark.org.uk | **Getting there** Free parking at Stonehaugh Picnic Site | **Tip** In a designated Dark Sky Park area, the Stonehaugh Stargazing Pavilion and Observatory is the perfect place to see the universe on a clear and moonless evening.

95_ Winter's Gibbet
Moorland murder

William Winter was a bad 'un from a bad family, no doubt about it. His father and brother were both hanged in 1788 for breaking and entering (or for stealing and selling a horse – reports strangely vary). Winter, too, had a criminal past and had spent seven years on a prison hulk moored in the Thames. 'Such had been the horrid depravity of William Winter', one newspaper solemnly reported after his final trial in 1792, 'that he had not been at liberty six months together during the last 18 years of his life'.

The crime for which Winter was tried in 1792 was the murder of Margaret Crozier. Winter, with sisters Jane and Eleanor Clark, murdered Crozier at Raw Pele, her home near Elsdon, in the mistaken belief that she was wealthy. When found guilty, all three were sentenced to death. And so, on 10 August, 1792, they were executed. Winter was hanged in Newcastle, and his body then hung on chains from a gibbet on Whiskershields Common, near the site of his crime. After their execution, the Clarks' bodies 'were sent to the surgeons' hall for dissection, and afterwards interred'.

Winter's corpse remained hanging for a number of years before his decayed body was finally cut down. Eventually, too, the gibbet rotted, and was replaced by a replica in 1867 by Walter Trevelyan, owner of Wallington estate. A wooden mannequin was added to complete the effect, though this was soon stolen. Since then, a head has represented Winter's mortal remains, though this too is frequently snaffled and replaced in turn.

A number of legends grew up around the gibbet. One is that a splinter of the original gibbet would cure a toothache when rubbed on the tooth. Another has the moorland nearby haunted by the ghost of Winter. Or possibly it's the spirit of a shepherd boy who helped bring Winter to justice, and who died in constant fear of reprisals a few short years later.

Address Elsdon, Northumberland, NE61 4LE | Getting there Free parking at Harwood
Forest lay-by opposite Winter's Gibbet | Tip Very close to Winter's Gibbet is the socket
stone of Steng Cross, all that remains of an Anglo-Saxon monument that marked the
highest point of an old drove road between markets in England and Scotland.

96 Armstrong Cottages
Dunworkin'

William George Armstrong definitely earned his place in history. He was born in 1810 in Shieldfield to Ann and William, who was a corn merchant in Newcastle. Armstrong was persuaded by his father to pursue a career as an attorney. He was subsequently articled to Armorer Donkin, a solicitor friend of the family who was like a second father to Armstrong and his elder sister, Anne.

However, science and engineering were young Armstrong's real interests. In the first three years of the 1840s, Armstrong developed his 'Hydroelectric Machine' that, although commercially unsuccessful, led to the creation of a hydraulic crane. This was installed on the Newcastle quayside and significantly reduced the amount of time it took to load and unload cargoes from ships.

This was the start of Armstrong's career as an entrepreneurial engineer. In 1845 he left the law firm of Donkin, Stable and Armstrong (he was made a partner in 1835) to found W. G. Armstrong & Company on Tyneside. Over the course of his long life, he would amass a huge fortune from armaments and warships. His company also built the hydraulic pumping engines still used to rotate the Swing Bridge in Newcastle.

In 1863, Armstrong bought a tract of land north of the village of Rothbury. There he had a huge country house built in the Tudor revival style, which he named Cragside. It was at Cragside that Armstrong entertained the likes of the Prince and Princess of Wales, and it was where he died at the age of 90 on 27 December, 1900. Cragside is now owned and run by the National Trust, and has been open to the public since 1979. Far smaller in scale are the Armstrong Cottages in Rothbury itself. These 12 almshouses were originally built for retired Cragside estate workers. Touchingly, they were dedicated by Armstrong to the *Memory of Anne Armstrong his much loved mother MDCCCXCVI.*

Address Rothbury, Northumberland, NE65 7NU | Getting there Bus 15, 16A, 16B or X14 Max to Queen's Head, parking on High Street and Front Street | Hours Viewable from the outside only | Tip The Coquetdale Art Gallery is a community gallery and studio where you can take part in a range of art-related classes or see the work of local artists. on display (www.coquetdalearts.co.uk).

97 _ Carter Bar

Scots Wha Hae

Drive northwards on the A68 and you'll eventually reach Carter Bar and the border between England and Scotland. Unlike other international borders, there is no need to show a passport or make a customs declaration. You don't even need to stop. You are free to cross at any time of day, as many times as you like. England and Scotland made peace with each other centuries ago, and so the border is an interesting waypoint, rather than a bureaucratic barrier.

A friendly, give-and-take, good-natured rivalry still exists between the two, of course. This was perfectly encapsulated by *The Jocks and the Geordies*, a weekly comic strip that ran between 1975 and 1990 in *The Dandy*. Both the Jocks and the Geordies went to school in the fictional border town of Crosspatch. During their encounters, the rival gangs attempted to outdo each other in often comically violent ways, much to the frustration of their teachers, Mr McAllistair and Mr Bigglesthwaite.

The strip could never be accused of realism, however. The Jocks wore tartan Tam O'Shanters so large that seeing anything other than their own feet would have been difficult. The Geordies favoured blazers and shorts, which is not a sartorial combination usually associated with the region.

The Dandy was produced by Scottish publisher DC Thomson. Despite this, it was the Geordies who invariably won. Newcastle-based *Viz* – 'Britain's third (or possibly fourth) funniest magazine' – regularly parodies the type of comic strip found in *The Dandy* and its stablemate *The Beano*. After one particularly scurrilous effort in 1995, DC Thomson responded with a one-off return of *The Jocks and the Geordies*, in which the two gangs competed to see who could produce the funniest comic. In this encounter the Jocks definitively win, with the Geordies suffering numerous indignities including 'being biffed on the chin by the triumphant Scots'.

Address Off the A68, Scottish Borders, TD8 6PT | Getting there Bus 131 to Carter Bar summit; free parking at Carter Bar | Tip Jedburgh is the first major town on the A68 when travelling through the Scottish Borders from Carter Bar. A particular highlight is Jedburgh Abbey, which is relatively intact despite being set ablaze by the Earl of Surrey in 1523 (Abbey Bridge End, Jedburgh, Scotland, TD8 6JQ, www.historicenvironment.scot).

98 Saltpan Rocks

Geology with a twist

A single human lifetime is a vanishingly small thing indeed compared with the vast span of Earth's geological history. Even *Homo sapiens* is a relative newcomer in the scheme of things, as modern humans only evolved some 315,000 years ago. Compare this geologically short period of time to the age of Saltpan Rocks at Scremerston. The various layers of limestone, sandstone, coal and shale date back to the Carboniferous period, approximately 330 million years ago. This was a time of giant insects, fish, amphibians and very early reptiles. It was also when what would become northern England lay near the equator, below a warm, shallow sea.

The rocks at Scremerston are all sedimentary rocks, of which there are two different types: detrital and chemical. Coal and sandstone are detrital, formed by the deposition of sediments or detritus over time. Coal is plant matter turned into rock through millions of years of heat and pressure deep underground. Sandstone is entirely inorganic and is formed when tiny grains of silicate – sand – are compacted and cemented together by the weight of sediment above.

Limestone is a chemical sedimentary rock, formed from the calcium carbonate that leaches out from the shells of animals such as molluscs or corals when they die. Lime mud forms when a shallow sea is supersaturated with calcium carbonate, and this is exactly what happened at Saltpan Rocks 330 million years ago. This mud would eventually form the beds of limestone at Scremerston.

What's odd about Saltpan Rocks is that the layers aren't horizontal as you'd expect. They undulate in a series of graceful curves, with the upfold known as an anticline and the downfold as a syncline. These whaleback curves are the result of two tectonic plates colliding some 300 million years ago, the enormous force of which caused the rock at Scremerston to deform. All is quiet now – geologically speaking – which is fortunate for us.

Address Cocklawburn Beach, near Scremerston, Berwick-upon-Tweed, Northumberland, TD15 2RJ | Getting there Free parking at various points along the Cocklawburn Beach road | Tip An outcrop of the oldest rocks in Northumberland can be found near a bridge over a stream north east of Makendon Farm in Upper Coquetdale. These rocks are shales, and were formed some 425 million years ago during the Silurian Period.

99 Farne Islands
For the birds

Northumberland's long, open beaches rarely get crowded, even at the height of summer. This is far from true on the Farne Islands, however. From late spring onwards, the islands are thick with hundreds of thousands of seabirds, there to breed. Commonly seen are species such as Arctic tern, razorbill, common guillemot, black-legged kittiwake and Eider duck.

By far the most charismatic of the Farne Island's summer visitors is the Atlantic puffin, known locally as a 'Tommy Noddy'. The most distinctive features of these delightfully loveable creatures are their large multi-coloured bills and bright orange legs. This slightly comical combination has also earned them the nicknames of 'sea parrot' and, perhaps more unkindly, 'clowns of the sea'.

When a pair of puffins come together to breed, they first dig a burrow in which the female will lay a single egg. The resulting chick, known as a puffling, is reared by both parents. Pufflings are fed on a variety of fish, including herring and sandeel. Parental puffins can often be seen with fish dangling down from their bills, up to 10 or 12 at a time. This ensures a good feed for the puffling, who fledge one to two months after hatching.

Life isn't easy for a puffling. When they first leave the burrow, they do so at night to avoid predators. They then spend four or five years at sea before returning to the islands as adults to breed. Although protected in the British Isles, puffins are still hunted on the Faroe Islands. In Iceland, the raw heart of a puffin is considered a tasty delicacy, and the bird is commonly found on restaurant menus. Puffin numbers are also affected by changes in environment. A drop in available fish can severely affect breeding success, and predators such as cats or mink can do serious damage to puffin populations. Puffins are a red-listed bird species, indicating an urgent need for preservation. To lose the clown of the sea *really* would be no laughing matter.

Address Off the Northumberland coast near Seahouses, NE68 7RN | **Getting there** Trips to the Farne Islands can be booked through the various ferry operators who sail from Seahouses harbour | **Hours** During the summer months only | **Tip** Boat trips around Coquet Island – another wildlife haven off the Northumbrian coast – can be booked at Amble Harbour.

100 Seahouses

Working hard at having fun

The coastal village of Seahouses is the closest Northumberland has to Blackpool. It's where you can buy sticks of rocks, wall plaques with amusing aphorisms, beachwear, novelty postcards, buckets and spades, and cuddly toys. Admittedly, there are no rollercoasters or illuminations, no Madame Tussauds or a Sea Life Centre, but there is crazy golf, the best fish and chips in the county, welcoming pubs, and the nearby beach is long and sandy and golden.

Tourism is the main driver of Seahouses' economy, but it wasn't always thus. Seahouses isn't even that old in the scheme of things either. It owes its origins to North Sunderland, just a short drive inland. North Sunderland was a fishing village, established at a time when Viking raids along the Northumbrian coast were all too common. Because North Sunderland was some way inland, villagers had time to prepare whenever an attack from the North Sea was likely.

In 1786, the natural harbour was improved by the building of a stone jetty, courtesy of the trustees of the Lord Crewe estate. The jetty meant that greater numbers of fish could be landed, and also made the exporting of coal and lime easier and more lucrative. Increasing wealth led to the building of homes along the sea front. These 'sea houses' eventually became Seahouses, the new village gradually but decisively eclipsing the older settlement.

Seahouses boomed during the Victorian period. At one point 50 herring boats regularly sailed from the harbour and, by 1855, there were six herring yards and associated smokehouses. So brisk was trade that in 1886 work began on the construction of Long Pier and New Harbour. However, during the second half of the 20th century, the importance of fishing declined. Fishing boats still sail into Seahouses, but increasingly they are filled not with herring but with happy day trippers loaded down with souvenirs.

Address Seahouses, Northumberland, NE68 7SJ, www.seahouses.org | Getting there
Bus 418 or X18 Max to King Street; paid parking at Seafield Car Park or Harbour Parking
Lot | Tip The wonderfully quaint Gunpowder House on the coast near Seahouses was built
to store explosives used during the construction of Long Pier and New Harbour.

101 Charlie's Garden

The one and only

A sea stack is a pillar of rock, formed when the sea and wind erode a gap in the cliff of a coastal headland. Eventually, the sea stack is itself eaten away, often toppling into the sea in a dramatic and noisy crash of falling rock. Northumberland has relatively few coastal cliffs, and so sea stacks are vanishingly rare. In fact, there's only one of note: Charlie's (or Charley's) Garden, a squat column of orange sandstone.

The rather charming – if quirky – name is thought to honour a Mr Charles Dockwray. Dockwray was a local villager who, according to popular belief, maintained a garden on the rock in the early 19th century, when it was still attached to the mainland. Since its separation, Charlie's Garden has been gradually whittled away. Today it is barely a stump, and may not exist in a century or two. For the moment, though, Charlie's Garden is the perfect place for seabirds to roost. Common visitors to the rock are cormorants, often seen standing eerily still with their wings outstretched as they dry off after diving for fish.

Charlie's Garden would have been a less peaceful home on 15 April, 1911, the day a paddle trawler named *Lily* foundered on the rock. *Lily* was built and registered in North Shields in 1888. At the time of the accident, she was owned by James Stephenson and Co. and, rather unfortunately, had been 'extensively overhauled' the previous month. On the fateful day *Lily* was 'on her way north to fish'. Oddly though, the sea was smooth and the weather ideal. Why she ran aground on Charlie's Garden is curiously unexplained. A reporter for the *Shields Gazette* speculated at the time that a strong westerly wind was to blame. Although the crew of seven were all rescued safely, they never gave their side of the story to the press. Badly holed, *Lily* remained stuck for several days during which time 'she was an object of much interest' to visitors.

Address Collywell Bay Road, Seaton Sluice, NE26 4QZ | Getting there Bus 58, 308 or 309 Cobalt & Coast to Millway; limited on-street parking on Collywell Bay Road | Tip The nearby Melton Constable is a popular traditional pub serving a wide range of drinks, including six real ales, and boasting an extensive menu of hearty pub food (www.themeltonconstable.co.uk).

102 Starlight Castle
All in a day's work

Sir Francis Blake Delaval was a card and no mistake. As a child he was an enthusiastic practical joker, encouraged by his fun-loving father and 11 younger siblings. Guests at Seaton Delaval Hall could find themselves suddenly thrown into a tank of cold water during the night, when their specially modified four poster bed was lowered through the floor. Or the walls of their room could be raised as they were undressing, revealing their nakedness to a crowd of sniggering onlookers.

Adulthood didn't improve Delaval's character. He was a spendthrift and frequently in debt. He was also an incorrigible womaniser, and liked to keep a mistress or two cunningly hidden on his estate. In 1750 he was all set to entertain a lady from out of the county. However, she would need somewhere discreet to stay but – irritatingly! – there was nowhere free. For Delaval, the solution was simple: build a castle and build it quickly. Samuel Foote, an actor and friend of Delaval, mocked his plan. So Delaval wagered 100 guineas that he could have a castle built in a day and before the month was out. In short order, the men of Delaval's estate completed the task in the allotted time, building the castle overnight by the light of the stars and so inspiring its name.

Is the legend true, however? Probably not. Starlight Castle was referred to as Sterling or Starling Castle during Delaval's lifetime. And the castle – though small as these things go – would have been a challenging and time-consuming construction project. More probably it is (and always was) a folly, one of thousands built by the English well-to-do in the 18th century (see ch. 36). After his death, Delaval was described in his obituary as 'the very soul of frolic and amusement' who 'overbalanced a few foibles by a thousand amiable qualities'. Perhaps the tale of Starlight Castle – now largely a ruin and hidden by trees – was his funniest joke of all.

Address Holywell Dean, Seaton Sluice, NE26 4QL | Getting there Bus 58, 308 or 309 Cobalt & Coast to Roundabout and then a 15-minute walk; limited on-street parking on The Links then a 12-minute walk | Tip Seaton Delaval Hall has suffered misfortune since Delaval's time, with a major fire almost leading to its destruction 200 years ago. It's now in the hands of the National Trust and is gradually being repaired and restored to save the structure for the future (www.nationaltrust.org.uk).

103 Lock-Up House

It's a fair cop...

Midsomer Murders paints a pretty grim picture of village life. In virtually every episode there is immoral behaviour, sharp business practices, cheating, lying, and – of course! – bloody murder. Watch the show regularly and you'd come to believe that country life is nasty, brutal and sometimes very short. If Midsomer were a real county, it would have one of the highest per-capita homicide rates in the country, if not the world.

Stamfordham – in non-fictional Northumberland – is just the sort of place that would feature in *Midsomer Murders*. However, the village is a largely peaceful place, popular with folk from Newcastle looking to live somewhere quieter and more rural. Stamfordham is where DCI Barnaby would buy a house, safe in the knowledge that violent crime was more likely to happen elsewhere. Ironically then, what Stamfordham does have – what a lot of villages once had – is a lock-up house. Lock-up houses were built in the 18th and 19th centuries and were generally used to detain drunks overnight, or to temporarily hold petty criminals prior to their being brought before a local magistrate. They were the responsibility of the (usually) unpaid parish constable, in a time before the establishment of a permanent and professional police force.

Stamfordham's lock-up house is a sturdy one-storey stone building. It was built some time after 1838 at the request of Sir John Swinburne (after whom the Swinburne Arms in the village is named). Swinburne was a politician and landowner, who was insulted by a 'person' during a meeting in The Bay Horse pub. A constable was summoned but there was nowhere to put the uncouth miscreant. After this incident, Swinburne gave both the land and the stone needed to build a lock-up house in the village. Why an insult should have had such an effect on Swinburne is now unknown. But as crimes go, it wouldn't make for gripping TV.

Address Grange Road, Stamfordham, Northumberland, NE18 0PE | Getting there Bus 74 Tynedale Links to Grange Road or Village Green; on-street parking nearby | Hours Viewable from the outside only | Tip Just a few minutes' walk from the Lock-Up House is Stamfordham's Market (or Butter) Cross. Built in 1735, the Market Cross still retains its original roof timbers.

104 Rabbie Burns Statue
The Scottish connection

Robert 'Rabbie' Burns was an 18th-century Scottish poet whose work is still recited and sung today. New Year's Eve wouldn't be the same unless someone sang *Auld Lang Syne*. And Burns Night – on 25 January – is not only celebrated in Scotland but across the world too, with recitals of Burns' *Address to a Haggis* a traditional part of the evening's events. Despite Burns' universal appeal, the fact that there's a statue of him in Walker Park on Tyneside is slightly puzzling. Who originally commissioned it and why?

Burns lived his entire life in Scotland, only venturing south of the border three times – all in May 1787. The longest trip was at the end of that month, with Burns writing down the details of the journey in his diary. On 27 May, 1787 he crossed the River Tweed stopping first at Alnwick Castle (see ch. 4), which he thought was 'furnished in a most princely manner'. The next morning, Burns carried on to Warkworth, noting that the town was 'situated very picturesquely…'. On 29 May, Burns arrived in Newcastle, where he met 'a very agreeable sensible fellow, a Mr. Chattox, who shows us a great many civilities, and who dines and sups with us'. The next day Burns left 'early in the morning, and rode over a fine country to Hexham to breakfast', and from there carried on home to Scotland, via Carlisle. And that was that.

The statue of Burns was installed in Walker Park in 1901 by the Tyneside Burns Club, whose members were mainly Scots who'd moved to the area to work in the region's shipyards and factories. However, by the mid-1970s the statue was in a sorry state indeed. It was first moved to Heaton Park where it suffered further damage. In pieces, it was then put into storage. In 2016, an exact replica of the statue was erected on the spot where the original once stood, with the now-repaired 1901 statue put on display in the YMCA Walker Park Café and Centre nearby.

Address Walker Park, Scrogg Road, Walker, Newcastle upon Tyne, NE6 4HA | **Getting there** Bus 32 or 995 to Scrogg Road-Walker Park; Metro (Yellow line) to Walkergate and then a 20-minute walk; on-street parking nearby | **Hours** Accessible 24 hours | **Tip** Scrogg Road (and the Scrogg Road Social Club) is named after scrog, a now-obscure northern word meaning land covered with low bushes or scrub.

105 Warkworth Hermitage
At home alone

Being a hermit has its pluses. You get to spend time thinking about things without fear of interruption. You also always get to have the last word no matter what (though you do have to provide both sides of the conversation). And no one can pinch all the duvet during the night and let you shiver with cold at two o'clock in the morning. The downsides are the loneliness, the boredom and the long hours (there's no time off when you're a hermit).

Warkworth has a hermitage, one that was created by hollowing out a cave in a sandstone cliff on the north bank of the River Coquet (it can only be reached by taking a short ferry ride, run by English Heritage). It dates back to some time in the 14th century, during the period of Henry Percy, First Earl of Northumberland. Or it may have been built earlier or possibly later – no one can really say for certain. One origin story is told in the long-form ballad *The Hermit of Warkworth*, written by Thomas Percy in 1771. However, as romantic and poetic as the ballad is, it is entirely a work of speculative fiction. The hermitage may not – strictly speaking – be a true hermitage either. It was possibly more of a private chapel, where a priest could perform services for a select group of people.

The first of two rooms is the outer chapel, which has a stone altar at one end. Next to the altar is the carved representation of a woman, reclining in a recess and overlooked by a smaller figure. The woman is commonly thought to be the Virgin Mary, with the other figure being the infant Jesus. However, the woman is not in a pose usually associated with Mary, and the smaller figure may well be an angel. The passing of time (and the touch of thousands of visitors) has blurred the details on the figures, so they are now impossible to interpret accurately. Another doorway takes you into the inner chapel, which may have been where the (small) congregation could have viewed the service through windows in the wall.

218

Address Near Warkworth Castle, Warkworth, Northumberland, NE65 0UJ, www.english-heritage.org.uk | Getting there Bus X18 Max or X20 Max to Beal Bank Top and then a 15-minute walk; paid parking at Warkworth Castle (free to English Heritage members) | Hours The ferry only runs at certain times of the day and only on Sunday and Monday between April and October; tickets must be booked in advance at Warkworth Castle (see English Heritage website for details) | Tip Warkworth's footbridge over the River Coquet dates from the 14th century and has a rare example of a fortified bridge tower at one end.

106 — Church of St Mary Magdalene

Keeping it in the family

Take a tour around St Mary's Church in Whalton and you'll quickly realise just how important the Ogle family once was. A vault below the Ogle Chapel contains the mortal remains of a number of Ogles. There's Henry Bertram Ogle Esq., who was 'respected wherever he was known, for his modesty, candour and integrity'. John Ogle is also interred there. He departed this life aged 32 in 1831, a mere 15 months after his wife died in childbirth. John's touching memorial was created by E. H. Baily, who later sculpted the statue of Lord Nelson in Trafalgar Square. And then there's Lancelot, who expired on 18 February, 1564. His roughly carved memorial is thought to be the oldest dated gravestone in Northumberland.

The earliest Ogle for whom there are records is Humphrey de Hoggle, probably born in 1055. The Ogles were Anglo-Saxon or possibly even Celtic, and therefore may have expected to suffer loss after the Norman Conquest of 1066. However, according to Bernard Burke's thoroughly comprehensive *A Genealogical and Heraldic Dictionary of the Landed Gentry of Great Britain and Ireland: Part 90, Volume 2*, published in 1863, 'William the Conqueror confirmed by deed, all the liberties and royalties of his manor of Ogle in as ample a manner as any of his ancestors enjoyed in the same before the time of the Norman invasion'.

Just down the road from Whalton is the village of Ogle, named after the family. It was here that Ogle Castle was built on the site of an Anglo-Saxon structure. The castle is one of the oldest inhabited buildings in England, and was where King David II of Scotland was held prisoner after his defeat at the Battle of Neville's Cross in 1346. It's no longer owned by the family and is private property, so a quick ogle inside is sadly out of the question.

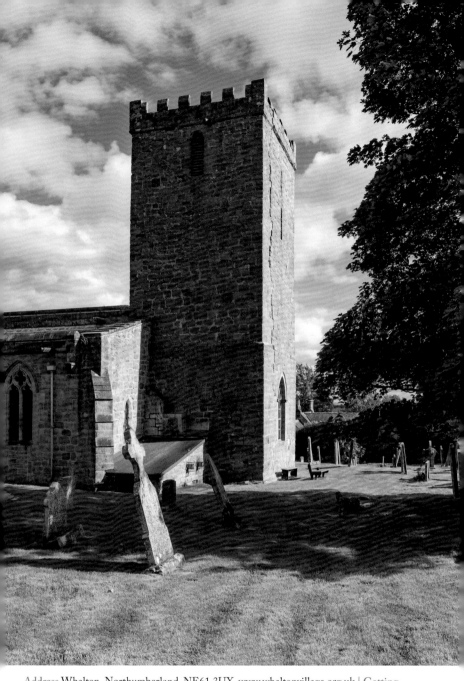

Address Whalton, Northumberland, NE61 3UX, www.whaltonvillage.org.uk | Getting there On-street parking nearby | Hours Daily 9am – 5pm | Tip Northumberland College Zoo is fun for all the family. Kids will love the meerkats and Asian leopard cats, and adults will appreciate the zoo's conservation and educational ethos (www.northumberland.ac.uk).

107 __ Whalton Baal
In the summertime

In Northumberland, come midsummer, the days are long and the nights vanishingly short. (The reverse is true at midwinter, but, at the height of summer, who wants to think about that?) The arrival of midsummer on 24 June is celebrated around the northern hemisphere in a variety of ways. Perhaps the most eccentric, however, is the Whalton Baal (or Bale), held in the village of Whalton.

The festival itself isn't that out of the ordinary. There's music, played on traditional instruments such as the Northumbrian pipes, as well as morris dancing, all of which is centred around a bonfire set up on the village green. (Baal is an ancient god, but the word is possibly derived from the Anglo-Saxon 'bael', meaning a great fire.) The village pub, The Beresford Arms, also gets in on the act, providing beer and barbecue food. What is charmingly odd about the whole thing is that Whalton's midsummer celebrations take place on 4 July. This is also Independence Day in the USA, though there is absolutely no connection.

The Whalton Baal is an ancient festival and has always been held on 4 July, as this was once the date of Midsummer Eve. This changed in 1752, when Britain switched from the Julian calendar to the Gregorian, which resulted in dates being moved forwards by 11 days. This is why midsummer is now on 24 June and not 5 July. Allegedly, the villagers of Whalton, being traditionally minded countryfolk in the 18th century, just went on celebrating Midsummer Eve on the old date rather than the new.

Fire festivals at midsummer were once common in Britain and across Europe, and probably originated in pagan propitiation rites to guarantee a good harvest. They largely died out in the 19th century when science took over from superstition. The Whalton Baal carried cheerfully on and has continued uninterrupted since its origins in the dim and distant past.

Address Whalton, Northumberland, NE61 3UZ, www.whaltonvillage.org.uk | Getting there On-street parking during the year, with more limited parking in place during the Whalton Baal | Tip In Allendale, the New Year is rung in by a procession of 'Guizers' carrying blazing barrels of tar on their heads. The flames from the barrels are then used to light a bonfire in the village square on the stroke of midnight.

108__Jam Jar Cinema
Preserving tradition

Although this may sound too good to be true, northern cinemas once accepted jam jars (or pop bottles) as payment for tickets. Eager children would take their (preferably freshly cleaned) glassware to their local movie house in order to gain entrance and see the latest flick. The cinema owner would eventually sell the accumulated jars to a local scrap merchant, who would make his money from recycling the glass. Alas and alack those days are long gone. The value of glass fell and the practice gradually died out in the 1970s. Take a used jam jar or two to your local Multiplex now and you won't even get as far as the popcorn counter.

The memory of these times lives on in the Jam Jar Cinema in Whitley Bay. Admittedly, old glass containers aren't accepted as payment. But the community-minded cinema does operate a 'Pay as you Please' system (the first in England, no less). There are three tiers of payment. Those who can afford to are encouraged to pay the top tier fee. This helps to subsidise the lowest tier, set at a level for those whose finances may be tight but who really want to see a movie. The middle tier price sits exactly between the other two for everyone else. And the wonderful thing is that the Jam Jar Cinema doesn't judge you for the option you choose; it's entirely a matter for you and your needs, or your conscience.

The Jam Jar Cinema was opened in 2013 by self-confessed cinephiles Dan Ellis, Stephen Fairly and William Smith. The first film shown was *Gladiator* and just 19 people were in attendance. Since then the cinema has expanded and now boasts three screens and a lounge bar. Wonderfully, the cinema has been wholeheartedly embraced by Whitley Bay and is now very much part of the town's cultural life. In 2020, the Jam Jar Cinema won the 'Heart of the Community Award' at that year's Northumberland and Tyneside Business Awards. And that definitely *isn't* too good to be true.

Address 16–24 Park Avenue, Whitley Bay, Northumberland, NE26 1DG, www.jamjarcinema.com | Getting there Bus 308, 309 Cobalt & Coast or 442 to Park Avenue-York Road; Metro to Whitley Bay (Yellow line) and then a short walk; free parking for two hours at Park Road Car Park | Hours Open 30 minutes before the first screening of the day until one hour after the start of the last film, Tue–Sun (see website for details) | Tip The Spanish City is a recently renovated Edwardian pleasure palace that once boasted the largest dome in the country after St Paul's Cathedral (www.spanishcity.co.uk).

109 __ St Mary's Island

All in a good cause(way)

Northumberland boasts two islands that – at low tide – join the mainland twice a day via a causeway. Holy Island to the north is by far the larger of the two but the other, St Mary's Island, features a lighthouse, something Holy Island strangely lacks.

The other similarity between the two islands is that they both have religiously themed names. St Mary has a special status in the north east thanks to her appearance in the region during the 11th century (see ch. 67). However, St Mary's Island was originally known as Bates (or Bait) Island as it was owned by Thomas Bates, a prominent local landowner in the reign of Queen Elizabeth I. During the medieval period, a small chapel was built on the island, dedicated to St Helen, mother of Emperor Constantine. Helpfully, a light in the chapel burned constantly as a warning signal for sailors sailing close to the island, making the chapel a precursor to the modern lighthouse. Confusingly, the light was initially known as St Katherine's Light but, for some reason, was later credited to St Mary.

During the 19th century there were a number of maritime accidents at St Mary's Island, and so it was recognised that a more prominent lighthouse was needed. Work began on the lighthouse and keepers' cottages in 1896, resulting in the demolition of the chapel. The first light was powered by paraffin and flashed twice every 20 seconds. St Mary's Lighthouse was electrified in 1977 and holds the unique honour of being the last of Trinity House's lighthouses lit by oil.

Not that electrification benefitted the lighthouse for long. In 1984, St Mary's Lighthouse was decommissioned and ceased to be a working lighthouse. It is now Grade II-listed and a visitor attraction. When the tides are right (check the timings before you cross the causeway!) and the lighthouse open, you can even take the Tower Step Challenge and climb the 137 stairs to the top.

Address Whitley Bay, North Tyneside, NE26 4RS, www.my.northtyneside.gov.uk | **Getting there** Bus 308 or 309 Cobalt & Coast to The Links-Cemetery and then a 14-minute walk; paid parking at St Mary's Island (South) and St Mary's Island (North) car parks | **Hours** Access to St Mary's Island and the opening times of the visitor centre vary according to the tide times; see the North Tyneside Council website for details | **Tip** Souter Lighthouse near South Shields is also worth a visit. Two highlights are the engine room and a restored keeper's living quarters (www.nationaltrust.org.uk).

110 Hagg Bank Bridge
The original Tyne Bridge?

There are two through-arch suspension bridges on the River Tyne, one of which is far more famous than the other. The more celebrated crossing is, of course, the iconic Tyne Bridge, opened in 1928 by King George V. The other is the Points or Hagg Bank Bridge near the village of Wylam. Hagg Bank is by far the older of the two, opening to rail traffic on 6 October, 1876. It was built by the Scotswood, Newburn and Wylam Railway company to serve the North Wylam loop line, which followed the route of the Wylam Waggonway with stations at North Wylam, Heddon-on-the-Wall, Newburn and Lemington. The cost of erecting Hagg Bank came to £16,000, or the equivalent of £2,362,000 today.

Despite the superficial similarities, the two bridges do differ in the way they were constructed. Hagg Bank has three arched lattice girders to the Tyne Bridge's two. The middle arch of Hagg Bank neatly divides the deck in two and is therefore a less 'clean' design than the Tyne Bridge. Otherwise, visually at least, both bridges are strikingly alike. This similarity may explain why the Luftwaffe tried to bomb Hagg Bank Bridge in August 1940. The bomber crew probably thought they were attacking the Tyne Bridge, which was a prime target throughout World War II. Fortunately, the bombs landed in a nearby field and exploded to little effect.

'The Reshaping of British Railways' was a contentious report published by the British government in 1963. (It's now more commonly known as the 'Beeching Report' after its author, Richard Beeching). The report called for the closing of underused and unprofitable lines and railway stations. Unfortunately, the North Wylam loop was one of those lines. In 1968, the final train crossed over the Hagg Bank Bridge, and the tracks were removed in 1972. Happily, the bridge is now used as a pedestrian crossing for people walking the River Tyne Trail or strolling out from Wylam generally.

Address Wylam, Northumberland, NE41 8JS | **Getting there** Bus 686 Tynedale Links to Memorial and then a 12-minute walk; train to Wylam Station and then a 14-minute walk; free parking at the Tyne Riverside Country Park and then an 11-minute walk | **Tip** Thomas Bewick was a renowned 18th-century engraver whose work is still fêted today. Born at Cherryburn in nearby Mickley Square in 1753, the original family home is open to the public, and many of his artworks are on display (www.nationaltrust.org.uk).

111 Stephenson's Cottage
Railway pioneer

Some people are overachievers. George Stephenson was very definitely one. Known as the 'Father of the Railways', he pioneered passenger travel by train, created the first intercity rail route in the world (between Manchester and Liverpool), invented a safety lamp for miners, and worked on numerous railway projects in Britain, as well as consulting on construction of lines built abroad.

It all started so humbly. Stephenson was born near Wylam on 9 June, 1781, in a two-storey cottage now maintained by the National Trust. The cottage is just a short walk from the village along the Wylam Waggonway, a tree-lined footpath that stretches from Wylam to Newburn. That Stephenson's family lived next to the waggonway is no coincidence. Stephenson's father, Robert, worked on the pumping engine at the nearby Wylam Colliery, and the cottage suited his needs perfectly. The waggonway was built in 1748 to transport coal from the colliery to Lemington, and from there it was shipped along the River Tyne to Newcastle. The waggons were pulled by horses until 1815, when early steam engines developed by engineer William Hedley replaced animal power.

Living in a rural cottage may sound romantic, but the noise of the waggons regularly rolling past would have been bone-shaking. The cottage was also divided into four separate tenements and shared with three other families. As was common at the time, Robert and his wife, Mabel, had a large family, raising six children in total, including George, who effectively all lived in one room.

Stephenson's parents were both illiterate, as was he until the age of 18. It was then, using money earned as an engineman at Water Row Pit in Newburn, that Stephenson put himself through night school. A gifted mechanic, and armed with his new knowledge of English and mathematics, Stephenson developed his first steam train in 1814. It was the first in a long line of achievements.

Address Wylam, Northumberland, NE41 8BP, +44 (0)1661 843276, www.nationaltrust.org.uk | Getting there Bus 686 Tynedale Links to Memorial and then a 12-minute walk; train to Wylam Station and then a 14-minute walk; free parking at the Tyne Riverside Country Park and then an 11-minute walk | Hours Viewable from the outside only | Tip The Wylam Railway Museum tells the history of the railway in Wylam (www.wylamparishcouncil.org.uk).

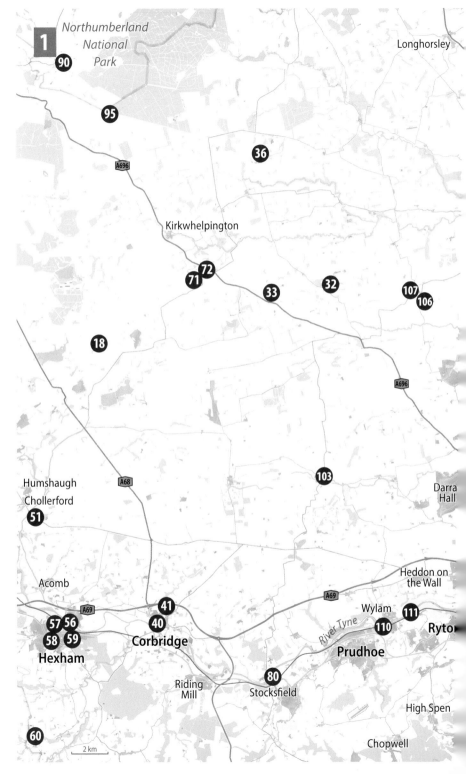

2 km

Widdrington

A1

A1068

A697

Ellington

45

Ashington
14
13

Newbiggin-
by-the-Sea
76

Morpeth
73 75
74

North Sea

Bedlington
20

Blyth
31

A1

Newsham
30

Cramlington
43

Seaton
Sluice
101
102 Old Hartley
109

42

Seaton
Delaval

47

Ponteland

Newcastle
International
Airport

Wideopen

A19

Killingworth

108

Whitley Bay

70

A696

Newcastle
upon Tyne
67

A1058

Wallsend
55

Tynemouth
North Shields
South Shields

Brockley

Fenham

River Tyne

Harton

78 77

Blaydon on
Tyne

A1

Gateshead

Whickham

Wardley

104 Hebburn

Jarrow

Boldon
Colliery

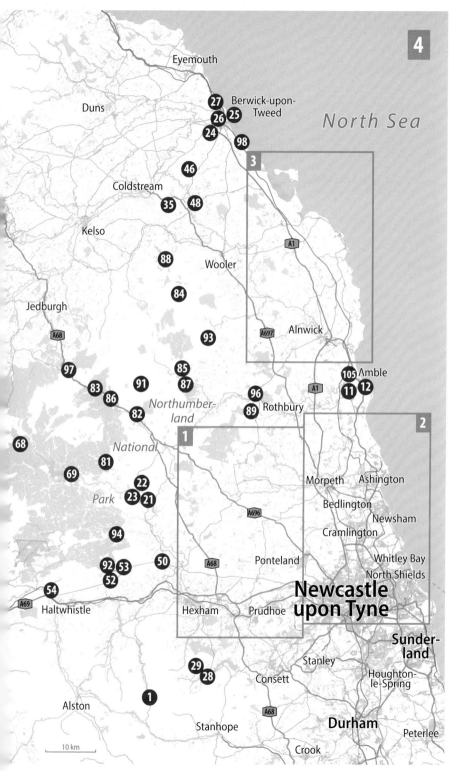

David Taylor
**111 Places along Hadrian's Wall
That You Shouldn't Miss**
ISBN 978-3-7408-1425-0

David Taylor
**111 Places in Newcastle
That You Shouldn't Miss**
ISBN 978-3-7408-1043-6

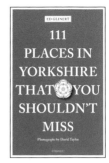

Ed Glinert, David Taylor
**111 Places in Yorkshire
That You Shouldn't Miss**
ISBN 978-3-7408-1167-9

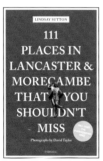

Lindsay Sutton, David Taylor
**111 Places in Lancaster
and Morecambe
That You Shouldn't Miss**
ISBN 978-3-7408-1557-8

Solange Berchemin
**111 Places in the Lake District
That You Shouldn't Miss**
ISBN 978-3-7408-0378-0

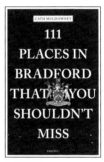

Cath Muldowney
**111 Places in Bradford
That You Shouldn't Miss**
ISBN 978-3-7408-1427-4

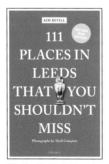

Kim Revill, Alesh Compton
**111 Places in Leeds
That You Shouldn't Miss**
ISBN 978-3-7408-0754-2

Michael Glover,
Richard Anderson
**111 Places in Sheffield
That You Shouldn't Miss**
ISBN 978-3-7408-1728-2

Julian Treuherz,
Peter de Figueiredo
**111 Places in Manchester
That You Shouldn't Miss**
ISBN 978-3-7408- 1862-3

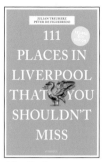

Julian Treuherz,
Peter de Figueiredo
111 Places in Liverpool
That You Shouldn't Miss
ISBN 978-3-7408-1607-0

Katherine Bebo, Oliver Smith
111 Places in Poole
That You Shouldn't Miss
ISBN 978-3-7408-0598-2

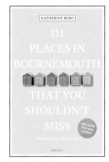

Katherine Bebo, Oliver Smith
111 Places in Bournemouth
That You Shouldn't Miss
ISBN 978-3-7408- 1166-2

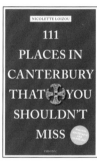

Nicolette Loizou
111 Places in Canterbury
That You Shouldn't Miss
ISBN 978-3-7408-0899-0

Rob Ganley, Ian Williams
111 Places in Coventry
That You Shouldn't Miss
ISBN 978-3-7408-1044-3

Martin Booth, Barbara Evripidou
111 Places in Bristol
That You Shouldn't Miss
ISBN 978-3-7408-2001-5

Alexandra Loske
111 Places in Brighton and
Lewes That You Shouldn't Miss
ISBN 978-3-7408-1727-5

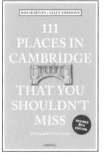

Rosalind Horton,
Sally Simmons, Guy Snape
111 Places in Cambridge
That You Shouldn't Miss
ISBN 978-3-7408-1285-0

Justin Postlethwaite
111 Places in Bath
That You Shouldn't Miss
ISBN 978-3-7408-0146-5

Gillian Tait
**111 Places in Edinburgh
That You Shouldn't Miss**
ISBN 978-3-7408-1476-2

Tom Shields, Gillian Tait
**111 Places in Glasgow
That You Shouldn't Miss**
ISBN 978-3-7408-1863-0

Gillian Tait
**111 Places in Fife
That You Shouldn't Miss**
ISBN 978-3-7408-1740-4

John Sykes, Birgit Weber
**111 Places in London
That You Shouldn't Miss**
ISBN 978-3-7408-1644-5

Solange Berchemin,
Martin Dunford, Karin Tearle
**111 Places in Greenwich
That You Shouldn't Miss**
ISBN 978-3-7408-1107-5

Nicola Perry, Daniel Reiter
**33 Walks in London
That You Shouldn't Miss**
ISBN 978-3-95451-886-9

Kirstin von Glasow
**111 Gardens in London
That You Shouldn't Miss**
ISBN 978-3-7408-0143-4

Laura Richards, Jamie Newson
**111 London Pubs and Bars
That You Shouldn't Miss**
ISBN 978-3-7408-0893-8

Emma Rose Barber,
Benedict Flett
**111 Churches in London
That You Shouldn't Miss**
ISBN 978-3-7408-0901-0

It would be impossible to write a book like this without the (often patient) assistance of others. For their help, I'd like to thank Nickie Hutton at Chillingham Castle; Kate Sussams, Peter Cumiskey and the volunteer guides at Newcastle Cathedral; Dan Ellis and the Friendly Team at the Jam Jar Cinema; Angus Collingwood-Cameron of the Northern Farmers and Landowners Group; Jennifer Whittle, Anne Moore, Charlie Barron and Becky Madeley at Museums Northumberland; Alison Jeffrey, Dave Richardson, Paul Buxton, Caroline O'Doherty and Rosie Thompson at the Northumberland National Park; Lucy Terry at Hexham Abbey; Ian McAllister and Ruth McGivern at Alnwick Gardens; Rob Mulholland; Trevor Gyllenspetz of CBRE Limited; Patti Purcell at the Kielder Observatory Astronomical Society; Dan Monk at the Gillian Dickinson Astro-Imaging Academy; Sonya Galloway at The Vindolanda Charitable Trust; Carmen Liegis and Chris Kelly at the Forum Cinema; and Ben Haslam at The Vault.

This book would also not exist if it weren't for the hard work and patience of Laura Olk at Emons Verlag and Ros Horton of Cambridge Editorial, for which I thank you! Thank you also to my parents, Bill and Carol Taylor for their encouragement. To Tom and Fiona for their friendship. And – last but never least! – thank you to my wife Tania, who shares my Northumberland adventures.

David Taylor is a professional freelance landscape photographer and writer who lives in Northumberland. His first camera was a Kodak Instamatic. Since then, he's used every type of camera imaginable: from bulky 4x5 film cameras to pocket-sized digital compacts. David has written over 40 books, as well as supplying images and articles to both regional and national magazines. When David is not outdoors he can be found at home with his wife, a cat, and an increasingly large number of tripods.